Ghosts of Madison County, Indiana

by
Nicole R. Kobrowski

Unseenpress.com, Inc.
Westfield, Indiana

Library of Congress Cataloging-in-Publication Data

Kobrowski, Nicole
  Haunted Backroads: Ghosts of Madison County
        Includes index
  1. Ghosts Indiana; 2. Paranormal Indiana ; 3. Indiana History; 4. Indiana Travel

Library of Congress Control Number: 2008930458
ISBN-978-0-9774130-4-1
ISBN-0-9774130-4-7

Printed in the United States of America

Published by
Haunted Backroads Books
an imprint of Unseenpress.com, Inc.
PO Box 687
Westfield, IN 46074

Although the authors and publisher have made every effort to ensure the accuracy and completeness of information contained in this book, we assume no responsibility for errors, inaccuracies, omissions or any inconsistency herein. Any slights of people, places or organizations are unintentional.

Cover design by Lorri Kennedy and Nicole R. Kobrowski
Text layout and design by Unseenpress.com, Inc.
Edited by Michael Kobrowski

All photos unless otherwise indicated are property of Unseenpress.com, Inc.

Notes

The persons, events, places and incidents depicted in this book are based on oral history, memoirs, interviews and accounts that were used as research for this book. The author makes no claim as to the veracity of the information. The author makes no claim as to the exact historical authenticity of the legends presented in this book. The author does not guarantee any location directions contained in this book and you visit these sites at your own risk. Although many sites are open to visitors during the day (and some in the evening), they all have owners.

Additionally, this book is comprised of material that is intended for the entertainment of its readers. The author has paid particular attention to collecting legends that have been told, in many cases, for generations. The information concerning these legends may not reflect historical events. The author takes no responsibility for the veracity of each story except that she believes the storytellers. The author has attempted to research each area as accurately as possible.

Although we made every effort to ensure that the information was correct at the time the book went to press, we do not assume and hereby disclaim any liability to any party for loss, damage, or injury caused by information contained in this book. Furthermore the publishers disclaim any liability resulting from the use of this book. The publishers and author do not condone, advise, or recommend visiting these sites without obtaining permission first and taking safety precautions.

We apologize if there is inaccurate information presented in the book and will rectify future additions and editions if we are contacted by mail or e-mail and provided the correct information.

Other Titles by Nicole Kobrowski

Distance Learning: A Guide to System Planning and Implementation
(by Merrill, Young, and Kobrowski)

Haunted Backroads: Central Indiana (and other stories)

The Encyclopedia of Haunted Indiana

Haunted Backroads: Ghosts of Westfield

**The following titles are published by
Kieser Verlag (Bildungsverlag EINS):**

Metal Line
Hotel Line (Instructor's Guide)
Englisch für Elektroberufe
Supply Line
Construction Line

Future Titles:
The Shadows of Central State Hospital: A Mental Health Legacy
The Encyclopedia of Haunted Indiana (2nd Ed.)
Ghosts of Indiana: Haunted Hamilton County

About the Author

Nicole Kobrowski is the co-owner of Unseenpress.com, Inc., which was founded in 2001. She and her husband Michael started the business because of their interest in the paranormal and their love of history. She has written professionally under a variety of pen names for over 20 years, including books for ESL and dozens of articles on a myriad of topics. Being a paranormal enthusiast for over 27 years, she has done investigation work in many areas including spirit photography, electronic voice phenomenon, and automatic writing. In addition to her work in the paranormal field, Nicole is an Adult Educational Consultant. Currently, she lives in her "über" haunted home with her husband and her semi-empty nested children.

Our Policies

We do not condone or encourage any type of harassment, vandalism, unauthorized cemetery preservation, or unauthorized trespassing. This type of thrill seeking only garners an unsavory pall over the paranormal community.

We are responsible in our investigations and research with integrity and according to scientific principles and standards.

We follow strict research and privacy guidelines. We reserve the right not to publish names and places contained within our books. Names denoted with an asterisk (*) in this book have been changed to honor the privacy of the participants.

We endeavor to create a true learning community for paranormal investigations with a collaborative spirit by partnering with responsible organizations that promote similar goals.

Acknowledgements

Special thanks go to the following people and organizations for their help with this book.

- The Alexandra Historical Society and especially Clifford Leroy "Pete" Sayre.
- The Anderson Public Library, especially Beth Oljace.
- The Fraternal Order of the Eagles 174, especially Bob Everett, Dixie Kirkwood, Tom and Peg Ferguson, and Tammy Ferguson-Blake.
- The Gruenewald Home, especially Jean Whitsell-Sherman and David Cagley.
- The Madison County Historical Society especially Steven Jackson.
- The Pendleton Library staff
- St. Mary's School and Church, especially Mrs. Nivens and Lavonne Stage.
- Kelly Marshall, for her friendship and support; Zac Wesco for his enthusiasm for life and everything in it; Liz and Carson Wesco for sharing sensitive information.
- Lorri Kennedy, for her artwork and wisdom.
- Mary Chapman, for her stories and 'tude.
- Michael Kobrowski, for time and support; food and drink; and honest feedback.

To my family ~ as always.
To my readers: Thank you for your complements and critiques.

Table of Contents

Preface

Madison County was my old stomping ground. I grew up in Anderson, close to Lapel and virtually had friends from every high school in the county. Even now when I drive through, visit friends, or patron businesses, I still remember the lazy summer days, the impossible thrill of movies at the Mounds Mall, Paramount, State, and Rivera Theaters. Although it's been almost 25 years since I moved away, over the last 12 years, I've taken my husband, Michael, to many of the places where I spent time. Every now and then, I remember another place and we'll traipse off to that location and Michael learns a little more about his wife, even after almost 17 years of marriage!

I am proud to come from a location that had such intimate Native American ties. Originally in 1800, the areas had a Delaware Indian village lead by Chief William Anderson, "Kik tha we nund" (meaning causing to crack, such as a tree in the forest). His son-in-law, William Connor ran a fur trading post near the home. Unfortunately, in 1821 the Delaware were made to move, mostly to Oklahoma.

I hated my history classes in grade school and junior high (sorry, Miss Meehan). They didn't make people in the past real. It was all a memorization of names, dates, and treaties. Love of history came much later when I moved to Germany and later moved back to Indiana. Now, I love perusing history for research. Without understanding history, we will never know where we came from, what we're capable of, or where we will go in the future.

When I write and research, I discover some of the most delightful tidbits that remind me even the pioneers were real people. Did you realize as far back as 1852 (if not further) that people were calling themselves "mediums" and sometimes shellacking the public? Don't get me wrong, I believe in mediums. I also believe some people call themselves mediums to buy money and attention. In the case of Mr. Ward McNear, his plan went completely wrong.

In 1852, a man named Oliver Branch, who was supposedly very rich, disappeared. People whispered that he'd been killed. For whatever reason, they said that Henry Huff, another member of the community, was responsible. Henry was smart and proved that Branch went to Fort Wayne, where he died of natural causes.

And the matter ended. Until Ward McNear, the self-professed medium, declared that he'd been in contact with Branch, He supposedly told McNear that Huff murdered him.

People went nuts. They wanted a lynching. They wanted blood. McNear, at the appropriate heightened moment, boldly and confidently stated that he knew where the bones of Branch were.

Over fifty people, armed with picks, shovels, and other digging tools, followed McNear to the appointed location. They labored into the night trying to find the murdered man's bones. Pumps were brought in the next day to clear out water that seeped into the site. Finally, about another half day into the dig, bones were found.

The pioneers readily identified them.

As deer bones.

Although the account does not say what happened to McNear, I can only imagine. Perhaps there were a set of human bones next to the deer bones after that day!

The days I spent in Madison County interviewing, researching, and investigating were pure joy. I love meeting new people and exploring new places. This book allowed me time reconnect with where I grew up and remind me of what is still good in Anderson. Helpful, friendly people full of pride and hope.

And for that, I am very grateful.

I welcome feedback on this book. This was a chance for me to get back to my roots and rediscover the joy of writing. I was blessed because I wrote the majority of the book in my home office which overlooks a weeping willow and pond. At times, I was able to take a break and watch the otters, ducks, geese, a blue heron, and other critters. I was also able to take a break with Bitty, a visiting hamster.

For some people, their recollections won't jive with what I've written. Undoubtedly, some folks will find a nugget of information I didn't include.. All is well. It shows we are human and that our history is wholly imperfect.

Madison County has in incredibly rich history and I am honored to be a small part of it.

NRK
June 2013

Names denoted with an asterisk (*) in this book have been changed to honor the privacy of the participants.

Early Madison County Hauntings

When I began writing this book, I thought the best story happened on September 21, 1891, the seventieth anniversary of the Native American exodus. On this night Kikthaweund was seen at midnight on the Anderson Hotel* (106 and 107 N. Meridian Street) with his arms folded and looking to the east. This was just as he was seen before he was forced to leave the area. On this second appearance, he faded into a cloud of mist in front of a dozen witnesses. Supposedly, his bones were found under the Anderson Hotel as it was being built and they were reburied there. He was also said to have been buried a half a dozen other places across the country. The truth may never be known.

But I found that there were a lot of other early ghost stories, only a small portion of which are included in this book.

In 1834 Mrs. Surber killed herself by hanging when her husband went to "muster," a yearly military drill that men between 21 and 45 were required to attend. She was convinced she'd never see him again.

Surber tied a rope around a beam, put her head in the noose and kicked a stool out from under her. When her husband came home, he took her hand and asked why she was in the position she was in. Her face swung around and he saw that her tongue was protruding and her teeth were deeply embedded in it. Mrs. Surber stayed that way for the next 24 hours, until the coroner could view the body. For years, no one wanted to visit the house because they thought they'd be "bodily captured by ghosts or spooks."

And again on January 26, 1896, the Anderson Herald published another haunting near Florida, Indiana. The ghost of Isaac Osborne roamed the 43 acre land he'd worked in his life. He had a feud with his neighbor Isaiah Bodkins. Osborne told his wife never to sell land to or let Bodkins lease the land. He threated to come back and haunt the place if she ever did.

Not heeding his wishes, Mrs. Osborne rented 40 acres to Osborne's nemesis. Osborne's ghost began to walk the place from night to day. Witnesses saw a strange light coming from the fields at various times of the night. It got so bad people decided to avoid that area, driving out of the way to their destinations. When Bodkins stopped renting the land, Osborne's ghost stopped haunting as well.

Additionally, in Lapel in 1901, citizens reported the ghost of Daniel Adams returned to blame his wife for having him baptized in a piano box filled with cold water. The result was not exactly saving him, rather he caught his death from pneumonia. Reportedly, his wife told him that she would move out of their cabin if he didn't stop haunting her.

Another haunting occurred in 1853 at the height of the Spiritualist movement. A mother sat in her chair and heard rapping on the door. When she said "Come in," no one came in. She went to the door but no one was there. When she told her family about it later, it began again, but no one could explain it.

That night, the rapping followed Sarah, who was 10 and Jane, who was 12. It started on their bed and followed them many places. Finally they sat down and tried to figure out who it was.

Using the alphabet and tappings, much information was provided by the spirit. Ollie Branch was one name of a person who said he'd been killed. Another was Thomas Quick, who died of smallpox in Ohio. This kept on for many months.

Finally, at the last meeting something occurred to make it the last. Several people in the area came to the meeting. Sarah was the medium. The house was fully lighted (which is completely different than what people do today– I disagree with having to "go dark"). The rapping began and the name "DAEVIL" was spelled out. The father took over and asked where he could see the devil. After many locations were discarded through the rapping, the "daevil" agreed meet him behind the house.

Sarah's father went outside to the back of the house. But he soon returned stating, "I did not see the devil. It must be too cold for the old boy."

The rapping began again and Sarah was able to guide a table around the room with two fingers. Her father asked, "Will you give me a ride, devil?" and he asked if Jim, his friend, could go with him. They got on the table, large men they were, and the men glided across the table.

Someone said the devil couldn't do anything in the presence of a bible, so one was placed on the table. Someone said "Shake it, old boy." as the table began to move again. The bible moved from side to side but would not be shaken off. When the bible was removed, the table began to become more violent.

The girl's father said they were never to play with the spirits again. They tried but the rapping followed them for many years.

Finally the rappings stopped and the girls lived long, healthy lives full of children and grandchildren. They attended church regularly but they often talked of the odd times over the years. Personally, I wonder if it had to do with them entering puberty.

Elwood seems to be extremely susceptible to the paranormal. A house that existed on North Tenth Street in Elwood was said to have a rapping ghost as well. Despite many people positioned to make sure the rapping was not coming from a jokester, they could not find a source for the noise. At one point, they actually saw glass in the windows vibrate from the rapping on it.

In 1903 an even stranger occurrence happened. In the southern part of Elwood, a small four room cabin seemed to be alive with consumption. We know now that disease spreads, but back in the day, people were puzzled by anyone who dare go into the building- and most came out dead. Afterwards, people believed the location was haunted and called for it to be destroyed.

Another Elwood house was believed haunted by Mrs. Anna McCleod who died in the home. It was unoccupied after her death and people claimed strange noises and figures roamed it. Finally, a family named Monanhan moved in on a Monday, not believing the superstitions.

By Wednesday, they started hearing noises that they attributed to mice. Later they heard a rocking chair squeak. Mr. Monanhan went looking for a prowler. When he reached the area where the noise came from, he saw a woman in a chair by the window and she looked exactly like Mrs. McCleod.

Mr. Monanhan grabbed his wife and they fled, finding lodging elsewhere for the night. The next day, they moved out. A seance was to be held later to speak with her. Later, the Monanhan's denied the reason they moved was because the place was haunted.

And yet another haunting was in a house on "the third lot north of North H Street on Fourteenth owned by Alemone Chaplin," Seven families moved out of the house due to hauntings. A man was found dead in the house, supposedly of alcohol poisoning. A year after that, a women fell down the stairs in the house. She was holding a baby at the time. She survived, the baby didn't. Family after family reported hearing noises and would soon move out.

John Marshall slept in the house and came out saying he spent a "terrible night" in the home. He heard the woman fall down the stairs.

But the earliest haunting I could find so far is from 1832.

In 1830 Mr. Abbott, his wife and his sons moved from Kentucky to Anderson. They settled near where the Moss Island Mill would be built. Their cabin was on the old Strawtown** road and it wasn't unusual for a traveler to spend the night with them. However, due to their somewhat reclusive nature, people thought of them as somewhat shady.

This theory was proven one day a couple of years later in 1832.

One evening, a man from Ohio was traveling through the Midwest looking for appropriate lands for his family. He told his family he would be back in six weeks. In eight weeks, his family began to search for him.

He was traced to the Abbott cabin. The family claimed he had stayed there, but moved on to the west early the next morning. Despite asking about the man further west, no additional information about the man was found. It was as if he disappeared- or never existed!

The Abbott cabin as depicted in "History of Madison County, Indiana" in 1914

Human nature never fails. Soon, a man's body was found floating in White River, close to the Abbott home. Because of public feeling surrounding the Abbotts, some people believed foul play was involved. Other people believed the traveler had just fallen in the river and drowned.

Either way, the Abbotts didn't stick around to find out. They packed up and moved out, never to be heard from again. The Ohioan was buried near the cabin. (I am not sure why the family didn't ask for the body back unless it was an issue of decomposition.) The one-person cemetery became called "The Abbott Cemetery." People began to believe the deserted cabin was haunted by the ghost of the unfortunate Ohio traveler. No one went near it at night.

Later, the land was subdivided and over the burial site was build a "cement house". ***

*In old city directories, the Anderson Hotel is listed at 106 and 107 Meridian Street. It was actually between Seventh and Eighth Streets. Don't confuse this with the newer one built in the 1930s and torn down in 1981 to make way for a bank which was never built.

**Strawtown Road was also named South Bank Road during the Native American days, Strawtown Pike, and most recently, W. Eighth Street.

*** The location of the house and cemetery is west of Daisy Hill Drive on W. Eighth Street. It is on privately owned land under an out building.

Gruenewald Home

626 Main Street, Anderson, Indiana

For many years, I drove by the Gruenewald Historic House (once called the Gruenewald Home) nearly every day. Either driving to or from school or attending to errands with my mother, I would see this beautiful home and wonder about it. Little did I know about its fascinating history.

Native American burial grounds are located on this property. Although the official story is that they are under the parking lot to the south of the house, early maps show this to be untrue. The burial ground extends to the house and north of it to the apartment buildings that stand there. One legend states Chief William Anderson is buried there.*

In about 1826** John Berry and his wife Sally, who were a founding member of "Andersontown" (Wapiminskink, meaning "place of the Chestnut Tree,"), gave 30 acres to the Madison County commissioners with the understanding that Anderson would be the county seat.

A short time later, Alfred Makepeace purchased one of the donated lots and constructed a log cabin and brick house with a shed roof. Today these rooms are the kitchen and dining room of the home with lofts above them.

The front of the home was remodeled in the French Second Empire style by Moses Cherry, a saddle and harness maker, in 1870-71. In 1873 an economic depression left Cherry destitute and he sold the house to Martin Gruenewald, who completed the house.

One of the most interesting features are the double doors and "coffin corners" on the stairway. He deliberately purchased the double doors to the house and made "coffin corners" on the stairway to make sure coffins could be taken in and our with ease.

Gruenewald has his own fascinating history. Gruenewald (meaning "green forest") came to America from Darmstadt, Germany. He settled in Chilicothe, Ohio in 1839. He spent some time out west and later moved to Connersville in 1861. It was here that he met his wife, Wilhelmina Christina (Dick) who was born in Wurtemberg, Germany.

According to Martin Gruenewald's autobiography, he came to America with $3.00 in his pocket. After his success from time to time, he would loan money to people in need, including James Whitcomb Riley. During Prohibition he stopped serving alcohol, although in his German heritage, alcohol was not looked upon as an evil. He was truly immersed in the American spirit and would not allow German to be spoken by his children in the house. He still spoke German to his wife.

One of his family members said of Martin, "His word is as good as his bond." Unfortunately for him, many of these people he loaned money to never returned it. And when he bought the home in 1873, he put it in his wife's name. Whether it is because she was leery of his money practices or whether it was something nice he did for Wilhelmina, is unclear.

Gruenewald married in 1866 and wanted to open a brewery in Anderson. He and his wife had three daughters and two sons. When he couldn't get the necessary permits due to some pretty determined temperance women, he opened a tasting room and billiard parlor instead.

Wilhelmina Gruenewald died at 49 of a lung disease in 1889. Martin resided alone in the large home after her death until his own death on November 27, 1933. Some accounts say he never really got over her death.

Martin's funeral was held in the house and presided over by a minister from the German Lutheran Church.

After he died, the house had a varied life. His daughter Clara, who had lived with him after her own husband died, kept the house and died in the parlor of the Spanish flu in 1917. It was used as a pet hospital, grocery store, and hair salon. It also had several owners and sponsors that saved it from razing over the years. These organizations included the Urban Development Commission, the Anderson Parks Department, the Lilly Foundation, community organizations and many individuals.

Currently, a volunteer Board of Directors maintains the home and carriage house (purchased in 1996). It houses an exciting museum and throughout the year, the home hosts many special events open to the public. It can also be rented for occasions. Due to the efforts of many, it continues to be a shining jewel, in the overly modern, parking-lot riddled downtown.

However, this jewel has a less brilliant side. Ever since I was a child, I was told the house was haunted. When one would drive by it, the home oozed history, but it also oozed spooky. With its heavily mansard roof line, each window in the home seems to have an eyebrow

Martin Gruenewald in his older years. (Photo courtesy of the Madison County Historical Society)

The piano Frank Thomas used to hide under in the "spooky" house.

cocked at its visitors. The raised entrance with ornate double doors seems to welcome visitors into its yawning recesses.

And it doesn't disappoint. In addition to the bevy of antiques and glorious architecture, people see and feel ghosts. Frank Thomas, the youngest of Martin Gruenewald's nine grandchildren said when he lived in the house that it was "spooky". In fact, he used to act like he stomped up stairs and then come back down and hide under the piano when everyone thought he was asleep. When someone else would go upstairs, he'd sneak behind them and run into his room.

Volunteers feel ghostly presences, and some don't want them to leave at closing time. The ghosts will position themselves in front of the doors, as dark wisps, trapping workers and visitors alike. Some people believe one of the ghosts is Wilhelmina Gruenewald because she did not want the home changed. Other people believe because this is part of a sacred Native American burial ground, that the restless spirits of the dead have come back to make their unhappiness known. One volunteer this happened to said that the spirit "swooped in like a black arrow of coldness", hovered over the doorway for about 30 seconds and then dispelled in a shattered pattern that looked like raindrops. These droplets fell to the floor, "absorbed into it and disappeared."

Additionally, an attic window is said to be home to an old lady peering out at the mission across the street. When we were on a bus tour, one of our tour members saw a woman in the middle window in the roof line at the front of the house. She did not fit the description of Mrs. Gruenewald, rather, she was a white haired, round faced woman who seemed to be curious about the activity. With so many people who have lived in and who have been associated with the building, this could be any number of people- someone who wanted to save the house, the Gruenewald children's nanny, one of the Gruenewald children, or someone who didn't even live in the house but whose possessions are in the house and she traveled with them.

Visitors and staff witnessed Martin in the parlor. And one board member's keyboard stuck every time she tried to type a "t". It would come out as "dt", such as in the German word "Darmstadt". It only happened after 3:00 p.m. when the person should have been out of the home. She and others believe it was Martin's way of telling her she needed to leave.

Stories don't stop at the museum. As far back as when the building was used as apartments, ghostly activity was reported. John, one of the tenants told his niece, Becky, that many evenings, he would lie awake and hear footsteps throughout the building. At first, he thought it was just other tenants- until the footsteps came into his living room. He jumped out of bed and searched the area, only to come face to face with a Native American. He was six feet tall, wearing buckskin pants and no shirt. Painted markings adorned his chest and face. And his face showed extreme sadness.

John asked the other man, "What do you want here?"

The man replied, "Justice." And with that, he disappeared.

John stayed a few more months in the apartment and took his leave. He only saw the man once, but for John that was more than enough. After the event, he made a habit of talking to the spirit before he went to bed, indicating that he was sorry for transgressions against his people, him, and his family.

John's experience brings up a question I've thought about for many years. I believe spirits are transient and can go wherever they want. They don't have to be tied to a specific location, nor are they always woeful in not knowing they are dead. I believe sometimes they do know and like it.

I've often wondered if ghosts are able to communicate in a different language than what they spoke in life. I am sure that the Native American in this story knew another language other than English. Did he communicate in English because he knew John spoke that? And he could speak English because he was dead and received this knowledge in the afterlife? Or did he learn it in the afterlife? My personal believe is that after you die, you know everything about everything. But rules exist for how you can interact and the information you can reveal.

The most intriguing paranormal experience happened to Sherrie who was attending a small party in the carriage house. The home was open as well during the time, and she took advantage of the opportunity to walk through it. She went through the ground level floor of the front of the house and up to the second floor in one of the rooms.

A woman dressed in a "fine, city dress" from the 1800s greeted her. The woman was in her late thirties, with brown, up swept hair. Her dress was of white and purple material, with black piping. She was carrying a matching hat with a large black feather. Her small, button up shoes were of a shiny patent leather. The woman was, "gorgeous, with an hourglass figure."

Sherrie was taken aback, because she did not believe the house

You never know who's going to meet you on the stairs.

had anyone except the party-goers and she said, "Excuse me. I didn't know the house was being used tonight."

The woman smiled at Sherrie and stated conspiratorially, "Oh, this house is always in use," and swept by her, giggling a tinkling laugh.

As the woman walked past, Sherrie felt the soft material brush her skin, and felt the wind of the passing around her. She watched the beautiful figure walk slowly down the stairs and disappear at the landing.

Sherrie rushed down to find her, but could not. She asked several people at the party and people running the event about the woman. No one had seen her or knew of any reenactors at the venue that evening.

Some reasons for the upheaval is the constant state of change in the building. It is old and there are always projects and restoration to complete. Some people believe this change and upheaval may disturb the spirits that reside in the house.

The second floor master bedroom has a mirror in which as far back as 1994 the staff would see Martin Gruenewald. "He loved to go to the opera house. He's dressed in his tux and putting his top hat on." according to Barbara Lumbis.

Carolyn Shettle, a member of the Board Of Commissioners in 1994, said that they heard typing in the upstairs office. When they got upstairs, no one was around. People have also gone upstairs and the hair on the back of their necks stand up. Shettle said she doesn't "believe or disbelieve... There are a number of things we don't understand and can't explain."

Sharon Joslin said a volunteer went to seek an explanation of noise when something moved in front of her and felt a frigid wind She couldn't move out of the room for a long time as if being restrained. Mediums who have visited report being in contact with Martin and his granddaughter Wilhemena.

For Martin Gruenewald, the Fourth of July was his favorite holiday. And no wonder, he refused to let his children speak anything other than English in the house. He and his wife would speak German, because it was their common language. Martin and his family would sit on the flat roof of the house facing the Norton Brewery and watch the fireworks.

David Cagey, the president of the board isn't surprised people believe there was a ghosts. People associated with the house have long believed items would move from room. He and his brother went through the house with his brother speaking German, but nothing happened for them. He believes the spirits, if their truly are some in the house, are pleasant. "Martin loved to entertain and he would want the house filled with guests all the time."

.
*Another legend states he was buried in Ohio or under the Anderson Hotel – or half a dozen other places!

**some sources have this as late as 1860 but John Berry died in 1835!

The Norton Brewery, where the Madison County jail is today. The Gruenewald Home is slightly to the north west of this picture. (Photo courtesy of the Madison County Historical Society)

Bronnenberg Home

(now Bronnenberg Youth Center)

Early in Indiana history, orphans and children, whose families could not or would not care for them, were largely left to be cared for through their own means, families willing to take them in, and churches. In the late 1800s, social movements began to right numerous issues with society including the topic of how to care for orphans.

On March 6, 1885, the Board of County Commissioners deemed that the children would be taken care of. On March 17, 1886, Decatur Vandeventer and his wife gave 10 acres as a site for an orphans home. It was on east Columbus Avenue and north 25th Street. The property contained a home already so it was an ideal place. During its 38 years of operation somewhere between 1,520 and 2,280 children were placed into homes.

In 1924, the Calvin A. Bronnenberg Orphans' Home was created, which afforded a larger facility for the children. Situated on the 256-acre Bronnenberg Farm, it could house up to 106 children at any given time. It operated until March 7, 1995. Now, the Bronnenberg Youth Center operates on the grounds.

The Bronnenberg family has a long history in Madison County. Frederick Bronnenberg, Sr, was one of the first settlers in Madison County (in 1819 or 1821, depending on the account you read). He is believed to have been born near Baden when the original family name was "Brandenberg". According to some accounts, Frederick and his brother came to America to avoid the German draft. Frederick was only 16 in 1791 when he made the trip. It is believed he and his brother changed there name to "Bronnenberg" to avoid detection by the German authorities

As Frederick and now his wife Barbara Oaster (Eastor) headed through Pennsylvania and Ohio, they eventually came to Indiana. Two accounts state different reasons why they settled here. One states that Frederick's oxen broke down and they stayed the winter and just kept staying on. Another account says a Bronnenberg child died and they wanted to stay where the child was buried. While I tend to believe the latter story, in 2007, an ox skull was found on the property and sent to the Department of Natural Resources for analysis.

Frederick began as a tanner, then opened a saw mill, grist mill, distillery, and a small woolen mill. All of which burned down in 1864.

Through the years, the Bronnenberg Cemetery would eventually hold at least 130 members of the family and the bodies of many of their neighbors. The earliest stones are for William, Frederick's son who died in 1836 and that of two infants from 1841 and 1842.

Frederick Sr. died on Aug 24, 1853.

His son, Frederick had 6 children one of which was Calvin Bronnenberg (born March 29,1852; died January 11, 1917).

Charles* who claimed to be a sometimes handyman the later Bronnenberg Home said that in the 1950s, the children would say that the home was haunted. Some believed it was by Calvin Bronnenberg, others believed it was the caretakers for the children.

Charles* told me that several children claimed when they were sleeping, if their toes were exposed, they would feel someone touch them or put a blanket back over them. Sometimes they would hear footsteps on the stairs and see a light glowing but no one would ever appear to see them.

He also related a story a little girl told him. She was about 8 years old and said she'd gotten up to use the bathroom well after lights out. She scurried to do her business and on the way back to her room, she encountered an older lady carrying a candle. The woman told the girl, "It's time you were back in bed." The woman escorted the girl back to her bed, tucked her in and walked away, disappearing at the door.

In the 1970s when the building was very old and run down, the general opinion was that it was haunted. Occasionally you could drive by and see the children playing outside. Even as odd as my childhood was, I looked at the children and thought about how much I wished they had parents to care for them. I often wondered if they went to school or did any of the same things we did.

A group of teenagers snuck in the grounds in the 1980s just to see what it was like. The area, right next to Mounds State Park, is a creepy area, full of vines, nature that seems to live and darkness. The house, imposing and darkened, lent itself to the event.

The kids approached the house, claiming they wanted to look around. When they got close enough to it, they saw a man come out of the back and start shouting at them. Afraid their parents would be called, they scattered and made their way back to their cars.

Jane was an unfortunate in the whole situation. As she ran toward the cars, her skin bitten by brambles, branches and "sticker bushes", Jane saw a glowing figure in the woods. She described it as "a white vision of a holy woman, so bright the light was."

The Bronnenberg orphanage has since been razed and the land where the house once stood is now the Bronnenberg Youth Center. The only parts that still exist are the arch that welcomed visitors (currently being preserved and not available for viewing) and the chapel. Permission must be obtained to drive into this facility.

Frederick's home on the grounds of Mounds State Park is open   for visitors- and is haunted.

This picture from about 1948 was a promotional piece for the Imperial Ice Cream Cone company. It showed good will and it also allowed the manufacturer to show other companies that institutions preferred their product. (Photo courtesy of the Madison County Historical Society).

The Bronnenberg Home. It was razed to make room for the Bronnenberg Youth Center. (Photo courtesy of the Madison County Historical Society)

This undated photo shows a celebration on the steps and lawn in front of the chapel. The Bronnenberg Children's Home is to the right.(Photo courtesy of the Madison County Historical Society).

Moss Island (Mills)

Moss Island Mills (razed) used to be directly on the river (about where Moss Island and Romine Roads are today). For many years because of the mills the Moss Cemetery was called Moss Island Cemetery. The mills provided meal and lumber for the inhabitants. Built in 1836 by Joseph Mullanix, it was preserved long after it was out of use. Moss Island was named because the flow of the river created an island and the fact that James Moss owned the property for a long time. Because of the mill, a small town grew up around the it. Subsequent mills, including a nail mill, sawmill, and gristmill also sprung up in the mile radius of Moss Island.

The eighth owners, the Traster brothers, Robert and William owned the Moss Island Merchant Flouring Mills, which made them very prosperous locally and throughout the country. They were very well liked and frequently hosted social outings on the island. Many people would picnic and fish from morning till night.

They employed a young man named Granville Dale, who used to be a "trusty" for them. Dale was a general manager of sorts, taking care of the teams, the horses and the mills. He would do errands and mill work and was trusted to bring cash collected for these errands back to the brothers.

During an April Sunday in 1867, a group of men assembled for a day of fishing. The group was in good spirits and became even more so as a canteen was passed amongst the group. The day wore on and the group, including the Traster brothers and Dale, finally heard the dinner bell and rose to enjoy the food. On their way, William Traster had a disagreement with Dale. Befuddled by drink, Dale picked up a rock and threw it, killing Traster. Dale realized too late that his employer and his best friend was now gone.

Dale turned himself in, was convicted of manslaughter, and was sentenced to 7 years in the Northern Indiana Prison at Michigan City. After he was released, he spoke of the incident with regret but also said he was a small man and Traster had been large. Dale was afraid of what Traster might have done if he caught him.

Moss Island Mill closed shortly after the event. For many years, the mill stood empty, a shadow on the merrier times that were had at the Mill. As time progressed, a family built the Morgan Breeding Stables close by– until a devastating fire burned the buildings and many of the horses. Today, the Anderson Transit System, Anderson Police, the highway garage, and other industries have a presence in the area where the mill used to stand.

For many years, a bridge ran from Baxter Street (Jones Street) across the river to Moss Island Road. I used to love to go over the bridge because it twisted around and there was a funky three way stop at the end of the bridge. I used to try for a glimpse of the phosphate covered river that resulted in masses of white, creamy bubbles. While fun to look at, the ecosystem damage was tremendous. Algae eats the phosphates and grow too quickly. The algae dies and blocks critical sunlight, in turn killing fish.

The area around Moss Island Mills is a very dark and foreboding area. The area around Moss Island Road and the Anderson Frankton Rd. is especially interesting. Strange creatures, too large to be native birds have swooped down on people. Apparitions of men in work clothes and women in prairie skirts are seen on the curve of the road walking toward Anderson..

In the early 1970s, the area was a place to party. Teens and young adults went out to the sandbars and listened to music, drank, and sometimes smoked a little weed. When this story was related to me, I thought perhaps the latter two items might have had some sort of effect on the story. However, the teller assured me the group hadn't been there long enough "for anything to happen." I'll let you be the judge.

"It was dark. The sun had been down for the better part of an hour. The regulars had just gotten there and were talking amongst themselves on the sandbar. We were faced west. I started seeing white lights coming through the trees. I just thought it was some more people with flashlights. I was next to Kit who was talking to one of the guys. I saw her go white, as pale as chalk. Again, I thought headlights or something was causing the effect.

She turned away from the guy she was talking to and looked at the whole group. Kit said, "Do you guys not see it? We need to get out of here."

At first no one paid attention to her, but when the light show started, we sure did. The lights I'd seen coming from the trees started swooping in and Kit, oh my god, Kit was just covered in this white light. She glowed. She held up her arms and kind of gathered the balls of light to her.

I could hardly believe what I was seeing. I looked around in shock. Everyone else was in the same state. Kit started talking. I don't know what she was saying; I don't even know what language it was. But she started walking toward from where the light was coming.

Suddenly I heard a pounding. It was like in cartoons when a giant is coming and you hear it take a step. The lights that were coming from the trees suddenly went into a flurry, moving toward Kit very quickly. And the pounding noise kept coming.

"The others around me had kind of snapped out of whatever state they were in and we were all looking at each other. We didn't know if it was the cops or what. For me, it was when Kit started convulsing that I truly got scared. The pounding got louder and closer. We saw a dark figure coming from the trees.

Well, it wasn't really a figure. It was more of a black fog. A fog that spread through the trees almost as if chasing the white lights. It seemed angry. Vengeful. Kit was still talking and the rest of the people were running back to cars, running on foot. I could see the sheer terror on some of their faces.

"I don't know why I wasn't more terrified myself. I guess I was just fascinated, despite the feeling I was getting from it. Kit moved her arms out to her sides and the light spread over the area. The pounding that came with the dark fog stopped and the fog itself reared up on the light. I could see it go around the light as if repelled by it.

Kit said something, I don't know what, and the light pulsed and the black fog was gone. So was the light. And Kit…Kit fell to the ground. I helped her up. She looked confused.

I realized how silent it was. Not a bird, not a cricket. Nothing. Everyone had disappeared. I didn't even know if the people had actually gotten into their cars and left.

"What happened? Where is everyone and where did that horrible man go?"'
What man?' I asked her.

"A man was coming out of the trees and he wanted to hurt us. I told him to go away."

I remember I kind of laughed and steered her towards my own car. "You did a lot more than that!" And I told her. We climbed in and closed the door. Neither of us said anything for a minute.

Kit locked the doors and said, "Get me the hell out of here."

From that moment on, she wouldn't go near that area, not even driving by in a car. She wouldn't talk about it either, for a long time.

Me? I never went back to party there. The group kind of broke up and some found other places to go. No one I kept in touch with spoke much about that night.

Years later, I spoke with Kit as she was getting ready to move out of state. She told me she was so upset by the whole deal because she had always been sensitive to spirits and such. That was the first time she'd ever clashed with them- and she doesn't even remember doing it. Kit was afraid it would escalate.

I never heard back from her after that. We fell out of touch. Maybe it's better that way."

If that wasn't enough, other folks who have been out for midnight rides on Moss Island Road or who have taken a walk at night have seen white figures on the very sandbar that the 70s party-goers used.

But not everything happens at night. A misconception is that "the witching hour" is between 12am and 3 am. Or that the paranormal is stronger during the night time. But there are a lot of paranormal events that happen during the day. Including one for Sandy and John, who do occasional paranormal investigations.

The pair went down to Moss Island and began to take readings with an EMF* detector. Getting no readings, they took some EVP** samples. When they broke for lunch they began to analyze some of the samples. At one point, John asks, "Who is here?"

The answer was a deep, laugh.

Later, when Sandy asks, "Do you want to communicate something to us?", the answer was, "Flat." That communication meant nothing to them until they went back to the car. Their tire was flat.

*Electro-magnetic field detector
**Electronic voice phenomenon

The old Moss Island Mill. Does the area hold spirits or something from another world?

Mounds State Park

4306 Mounds Road, Anderson Indiana

Frederick Bronnenberg was the first of his family to settle in America in 1800. By 1837 he'd moved his family to Indiana and had a sawmill. Later a grist mill, carding mill and distillery were also part of the family businesses. He and his wife Barbara had 12 children, 9 of which survived birth.

Frederick Jr, added the Federal style "ell" house which still stands in the Mounds State Park and his son Ransom made improvements to it. The property contained a spring house (whose remnants can be seen at the bottom of a ravine behind the home), corn crib, smokehouse, barn, and summer kitchen. After his father's death, Frederick continued to preserve the mounds, led groups to them, and told of their importance. After his death, Ransom was given the property and he continued the tradition.

During the Interurban height, people used to come to see the mounds as a destination spot. I remember as a child going to the park for field trips and seeing the unused railroad loop and wondering what it was for. An amusement park was added which deteriorated some of the mounds. A kiddie train went across the Great Mound. After the Great Depression, the amusement park closed the land was transferred to Indiana as a park.

Charles T. Sansberry, an attorney and president of the Madison County Historical Society, was instrumental in preserving what we know as Mounds State Park. At one time, land developers wanted to make it into housing additions.

To do this would have certainly destroyed 10 mounds and earthworks built around 150 B.C. by the Adena and Hopewell people.

The property proposed includes what was known as the Williamson farm with three mounds and the Bronnenberg land to connect the Union Traction Company of Indiana land with seven mounds.

The early Adena and Hopewell people seemed to have a trade system with at least beads, obsidian, seashells and mica for bargaining. Pottery for cooking and woven material for clothing and other essential items were also used.

They had a sophisticated understanding of a calendar system. The Great Mound was aligned to mark the summer and winter solstice and the spring and fall equinox. The Circle Mound was set up so that it aligns east and west with the diagonal alignments marking the winter and summer solstices. During the spring and fall equinox, the sun aligns with the mound's gateway. The Fomalhaut/Earthenwork B lines up with the star Famalhaut in the fall. The Woodland Mound/Earthenwork D aligns with sunset on the winter solstice. There are other mounds at the park with equally interesting stories and other mounds existed in the area, however early settlers plowed them under for farming and housing and allowed looters to come in and take artifacts.

The project hit a few snags when the landowners had a slight change of heart to sell part of it for commercial purposes. But eventually, the proposal went through in 1931, shortly after Sanberry's death.

Today, Mounds Park is a destination park for people interested in history and nature. It is a park that protects a cultural site and the park surrounds it. In the park, as you come around close to the Bronnenberg house, (not to be confused with the Calvin A. Bronnenberg Orphan's Home), a small mound is in the forest.

While on a field trip, the guide asked if we saw it and asked me to go stand on it. I was told that you never step on their burial sites or it causes bad luck. I declined with an emphatic shake of my head. No way was I going to stand on a mound. My own Native American ancestors might come and get me– and after the paranormal experiences* I'd had in my life so far, I certainly didn't want to rock the boat!

A classmate, Ross, gladly went out and stood on the mound to show its location. He did not pass eighth grade. And although people say it's superstition and coincidence, I still believe.

Dwarfs, known as Wemateguni*, live here. They are described as short people wearing glowing blue robes. This is interesting because the White River was a major waterway for the people of Madison and Hamilton counties. In addition to seeing these beings at Mounds Park, some people have reported encountering blue-gowned dwarves nearby along the White River at Noblesville and Strawtown. According to Indian legend, they are the Puk-wud-ies, a tribe of peaceful little people that still inhabit the forest. Many investigators have entered the park only to find that they've entered a time warp and instead of spending a couple of hours investigating, six or more hours have elapsed.

The Frederick Bronnenberg House at Mounds Park hasn't escaped ghosts either. Visitors and staff report hearing footsteps. Investigative groups have captured orbs. A shadowy figure peeks out the top

This is the Fredrick Bronnenberg home circa 1890. An unmarked family graveyard is supposed to be somewhere in the park. If you look closely at this picture, it seems to have tombstones behind the fence. (Photo courtesy of the Madison County Historical Society)

A 2013 photo of how the Frederick Bronnenberg House looks. Notice the fence- no tombstones.

middle window. Many people believe this is one of the Bronnenberg men.

Gerald, a nature lover, said he used to hike the trails a lot when he was mobile. One afternoon as he ate his lunch by the river, in the distance, he saw a small band of these people walking along the river bank. At first, he thought someone was filming a movie or there were reenactors for the visitors. When he called out to them, they looked at him, their bronzed faces looked in unison at him and they disappeared before his eyes.

Additionally, visitors have been out after dark and have seen various transparent spirits of Native Americans and white men. Two eyewitnesses were hiking in 1975 past the serpent mounds. The birds got quiet and there was a group of native men in the woods close to them. They gestured the couple over and one of them gave the woman an old bead, which she still has today. The men walked off and disappeared.

In the late summer evenings and into the fall, fewer people stay late at the park but some folks still camped out overnight.

On one such night, campers Sarah and Scott, paranormal enthusiasts decided to take flashlights and go on a walk. They had heard about some small caves and wanted to see if they could find them. Caves are so much better at night. These caves are not open to the public. Some stories state that in the 1920s a child was lost in one for several hours. Another story states that they were all dynamited in the 1920s or 1930s. Still another Internet legend states that a girl died in a cave in the 1920s.

Walking through the trails, Sarah and Scott became aware of someone following them. At first, they believed it was just another person spending the night at the park. They went off the trail to a place where they believed the cave was. Sarah saw something dart to the left of them.

She stopped and asked Scott if he'd seen something.

Scott chuckled, "I knew you'd get this way."

Sarah shot him a baleful look and continued forward.

A short time later, Sarah stopped again. "I know I saw something."

Scott sighed, "If you're too scared…"

Sarah said sharply, "I am not scared. Something is out here with us."

Scott teasingly said, "Yeah, another camper out to scare us."

Moving forward, they shined their lights on an outcropping not too far from a trail. They could only see darkness outlined by vegetation.

Scott stepped forward and grunted, "I think we found one."

From the darkness, three men stepped forward, their figures a dim vision in the glow of the flash lights.

For a moment Sarah and Scott were frozen.

"Leave." One of the men said.

Sarah said, "Why?" as Scott was moving away. Later Sarah said she didn't know why she said it.

"Leave." The man repeated and stepped forward.

Scott pulled at Sarah's arm. "We should...."

Sarah shook him off and stepped forward, "Were you the people following us?"

Another man stated, "You will leave now."

The way he said it gave Sarah pause for thought. It was then she noticed they weren't just outside of the light enough to make them dark, rather they were dark.

The men were about 5' 8" inches tall, and all that could be seen of their features were their bright whites and the brilliant grape green of their eyes. The rest of their features seemed to be shrouded in gauzy material.

"Who are you?" asked Sarah.

"I don't think you should have done that." Scott said pulling at her arm harder.

In an instant, the three men merged into one being and became the shape of a big, black bear. It growled at them, lumbering forward.

By this time, Sarah and Scott were stumbling backwards, frightened beyond words. They ran all the way back to their tent and zipped it up.

Looking back on the experience, Scott said, "I realize that wouldn't have kept anything out, but it gave us enough peace of mind to be back with the other campers at the time. "

For a few hours, they sat in the tent whispering about what happened. They tried to make sense of it. In the morning, they stepped outside their tent when they heard others stirring and it was daylight. Stretching, they agreed it was time to leave and find another, less frightening adventure.

One of the caves at Mounds Park. A girl was supposedly lost in one. And a couple had an unusual meeting with Native American visitors from the past. Some people believe these caves were sacred to the Native Americans and that the caves hold magical powers.

That was when Scott looked at the ground around the tent. Bear paw prints circled the tent, although they both swear they never heard anything outside of the tent once they returned. According to the Department of Natural Resources in Indiana, black bears do not naturally inhabit Indiana anymore.

Sarah reflected, "I want to think they were protecting us from something versus being evil. I don't believe just because it was a black form that it was bad. And with the connection of Native Americans and their connection to nature and animals, I believe we saw something in that realm."

Some people do believe that earth elementals were called upon to protect the place. These protect the place against intrusion because it is a sacred place. Perhaps what Scott and Sarah met was an elemental protecting the cave because it was special. For example, Cherokee use medicine stones flushed by water from caves. Cherokee pick them up outside the cave, but you can't take them from inside. A recommendation when going to Native American sites is to carry blue corn and tobacco with you and leave offerings as you go.

Lorri Kennedy, a reiki master used to spend long weekends in the park. She said "If you hike in there, you can see the Indians and strange creatures. Once when we were horseback riding, we saw four Native Americans come from the river, rising out as if they had swam or came covertly under the water. They looked to be Miami related, not with feathered headdresses, but with feathers in their hair. One had a partially shaved head, but not a Mohawk. One was about 5' 11" tall, the other was very tall, over six feet. They wore loin cloths to cover their manness. The tall one gave me a bead, but my mother threw it away. It was a rectangular bead, grayish blue color, maybe 3 millimeters in size, with very small linked circles. We weren't scared as kids, we just accepted it. It was like we were in a bubble of understanding."

She also witnessed a small humanoid about two or two and a half feet tall. "I kept hearing things and turning around. Finally I saw it. It looked human but the joints were more knobby. It has squinty eyes and a pointed chin." Lorri didn't remember any clothing on it. She says these creatures were there to help the Native Americans. "Tribes needed help in the woods. They would leave the creatures offerings and the creatures would help out. The Native Americans had a great respect for these creatures. It was a fine balance they had between giving the right tribute and not enough, causing them to trickster you."

In an archaeological report Donald Cochran and Beth K. Mc-Cord wrote of a dream that came the night before they finished a report for the Archaeological Resources Management Services at Ball State.

An old man with skin "the color of walnut" and his long gray hair pulled away from his face told the story of his people. He said he was the guardian of the mounds. The authors had been chosen by "his people" to tell the story. The old man said that the people lived and died there, that they had names for every part of nature around them, and that they were one with the earth. They celebrated, cried and took what was needed from the land. They gave back to the land as well and took care of it. The mounds created a greater connection with the land, the earth, the air and the sky. "They [people who came after the old man] should not be surprised that a simple people could create such a place, but to be impressed with the meaning behind it."

Other sources say these dwarves are Pukwudgie. The difference is that "Pukwudgie" comes from tribes who were not part of the area. "Wemategunis" comes from Lenape, who were part of Madison County.

Killbuck Park
(now Killbuck Golf Course)

The earliest, most pleasant memories I have of Anderson, besides running outside after a thunderstorm in my bathing suit printed with whales blowing their spouts, and throwing myself into the water running by the curb, involves Killbuck Park.

The park was purchased by the Delco-Remy Welfare association in 1955. Prior to that, it was known as the Gola Childes' Bethany Acres farm. Before it officially opened as Killbuck Park, Guide Lamp Division joined the venture. In the first two months alone, 40,000 men, women, and children visited the park.

As my father was an employee of the General Motors Corporation, families of the company could go to the park and enjoy miniature golf, walking, fireworks, cookouts, and occasionally, fair rides. Every year, we attended a company sponsored picnic, sometimes enjoying fireworks. We usually arrived shortly after 10:00 a.m., and didn't leave until well after dark. What my parents did during that time, I don't know. I was too busy exploring the woods, picking up the numerous shells on the sandbars in Killbuck Creek and running after my older sisters, wanting to do what they were doing. (And they were busy trying to ditch me– usually succeeding!)

I certainly had no inkling of the person that the creek and park were named after. Charles Henry Killbuck was a Delaware and son of Gelelemend, the Delaware Indiana chief. His Christian name came from baptism by the Moravian Church on May 21, 1789 at Pettquotting (near Milan, Michigan). He was called "Captain Killbuck" because that rank was given to Native Americans who helped lead tribes in times of trouble and who were considered next in line for chief. His Native American name was Chief Kelelamand, meaning "big cat".

In January of 1801, the Moravian Mission at Goshen asked him to meet with the Delaware on the White River. The Moravians wanted to send missionaries to work with the Delaware. Permission was obtained but problems ensued. Yet in 1805 he translated an English speech into Delaware and provided letters and Indian hymn books to them.

In 1813 after being directed by General William Henry Harrison to leave, the Delawares went to Piqua, Ohio but later returned. Killbuck's Town (aka Buck's Town)* was formed on what would later be the

Carroll Bronnenberg Farm. This was on a high bluff east of White River and just northwest of Chesterfield.

With the Treaty of St. Mary's, Ohio, he was forced to leave. He and his family moved to New Fairfield, Canada. According to local legend, despite his move to Canada, Captain Kilbucks' remains are buried somewhere in the wooded area, near the dam of the Killbuck Creek. This dam was put in place solely to allow water to penetrate the ground and replenish city wells. At one time, this land was the Sparks' Farm. Now it is Shadyside Park.

It explains a lot as Shadyside is covered in this book as well.

Indiana is full of stories about Native Americans and nature spirits. From wind and rain spirits to day and night spirits, Native Americans believe everything is related to spirits and they honor the spirits and the dead in many ways. In my own yard, I have a slate board with shells. Sometimes I burn sage or tobacco as an offering. It is my meditation spot.

For as long as I can remember at Killbuck, people have always talked in hushed whispers about the sacredness of the place. Whether this has to do with Chief Killbuck or the fact that the park has his name is a mystery yet to solve.

When I speak with others from Anderson who remember the park, they all have fantastic memories of the park, as I do. Fireworks on the Independence Day, company sponsored picnics, hanging out with friends, and the train that made endless treks around the park.

However, some people have other memories. The Killbuck Golf Course is part of the old park, but there is still a tract of land that is wooded near the creek. This area is where one local man believes he came face to face with a vision from the past.

When the park was still open to General Motors workers, Brad used to go out and hunt for rabbits and squirrels and collect shells. He ate the rabbits and squirrels and used the shells for jewelry. Brad tried to be conscientious and use all parts the animals. As a result, he had a couple of beautiful rabbit blankets. He did not only go to Killbuck for shells and he didn't try to upset the eco system. He would only use the shells that washed up on sandbars. Brad considered these "safe" or an "offering" from the nature spirits and therefore "ok" to use.

Brad remembered on one of his outings a very surreal experience. It was early spring and Brad was dressed in hip wader walking along the bank of the creek. He could still see some ice along the edge in the shade and he was keeping a watchful eye out for some shells. It hadn't been a super productive morning as he had no luck with rabbits, which was unusual for him. Usually, he was able to find a few burrows and make a claim on a few rabbits.

Today, it was quiet. Usually so. To Brad, it seemed as if the water "wasn't moving right." As he walked by the barren banks of the creek, he rejoiced in the warm sun on his face and enjoyed the trees which seemed to be hands reaching to the sky.

A movement out of the corner of his eye caught his notice. When his eyes focused, he saw two children chasing what looked to be a ball.

Brad could see them moving and hear their laughter.

And then he realized he could see through them.

And they were bundled in furs.

And the ball they were chasing was actually a bladder.

Brad didn't know what to do. He wasn't scared, "I was more surprised than anything. Killbuck had never given me any cause to be afraid."

The children continued to play and then faded out as they reached the woods. Brad was just recovering from that experience when he heard a gentle lapping behind him. His jaw "dropped to the ground" when he realized that a Native American in a dugout canoe. The man in the canoe was fairly young with long, dark hair, and also bundled in fur. As the man passed by Brad, he turned to Brad, gave him a nod and moved on. This canoe faded away as well.

Brad forgot about the rabbits and shells. He realized he was in some sort of time warp and knew how special it was. As if what he'd experienced wasn't enough, Brad heard a woman crying. He saw a short, dark haired woman bundled in furs. By this time, "I was so used to it, I had to talk to her."

Brad asked her what was wrong and she said she was looking for her family. "She was speaking a different language, but I could hear her in English in my mind." He told her about the kids and the man in the canoe. The woman wanted to know where they went. Brad took her to the edge of the woods where he'd seen the others disappear.

"A cool wind blew over, chilling me." Brad explained. "And suddenly, the man who was in the canoe was in front of me with the children. The man began to cry and the children ran to the woman. They embraced her. It was beautiful."

Time dilation is a fact. The basic principle is that (for example) if two people are living at different elevations, time passes more slowly or quickly, depending on the location. Experiments have shown that time does move differently but they add up to fractions of seconds and even over a lifetime, you would not notice the difference. Time warps have not been ruled out, according to Stephen Hawking.

Brad said as close as he could tell, this was a family that was separated somehow. They had been searching for each other for "many years."

"They turned to me, smiled and disappeared," Brad concluded. "Later, when I returned home, I found, tucked inside my shell collection bag, a small bladder with something in it. I deflated it carefully and inside, I found a beautiful water polished stone."

The site of his town was southwest of the intersection of CR 75N and CR 300E where the White River turns south west.

Fraternal Order of Eagles 174
1315 Meridian Street, Anderson, Indiana

The Fraternal Order of Eagles (FOE) is an international organization with a history of helping people and supporting community. In Middle America it has very deep ties as truly a social organization that takes care of its family and those around them. It is a not-for-profit and takes pride in making "human life more desirable by lessening its ills and promoting peace, prosperity, gladness and hope." The members of the FOE 174 in the Art Deco building on Meridian Street are no exception. They've helped raise money for a variety of causes and describe themselves as "people helping people."

We heard for years that the building was haunted. Walking into the building you are transported back in time. The lobby has strong elements from the 1940s, some earlier. A small museum is off to the left. The bar and common room have a homey charm where everyone is a friend. When we arrived at the building, I was told everything I wanted was "upstairs," by several people. Tammy Ferguson-Blake and her parents, Tom and Peg Ferguson, were waiting for us. We were still waiting on a few more people, so we sat around and talked for a few minutes. Everyone had a story.

The FOE 174.

Peg, who is absolutely fascinated with the paranormal, said that she's had a lasting experience. Her brother wanted her to go to the Medix Run Hotel (in Weedsville, Pennsylvania). Knowing it was haunted, off they went. They were waiting outside to be seated and Peg needed to use the ladies room. "It was an old, rickety building, so I had to yank the restroom door closed to lock it." When she left the stall to wash her hands, the door was wide open. There was no way for it to be unlocked from the outside.

Tammy, her daughter, also has had experiences. Her brother haunts her house, pulling pranks on her- much to her consternation. He takes her personal items and hides them. Once, the cough syrup flew off the counter and into the dog food bowl. Tammy said, "This started happing the day after he died." Once, when Tammy's son, Chris was sitting with his girlfriend in the living room, the ceiling fan began to rock. Tammy asked him not to appear to her and so far, he's complied.

She is also the same Tammy that many of you who have attended our tours may have heard me mention. My sister, Mary and I stayed at Tammy's house one Saturday night when we were teenagers. Her parents were out for the night and we were trying to figure out something to do. Tammy suggested the Ouija board. I started playing her parent's small organ in a creepy way and said sure.

When nothing happened, I suggested throwing a bible on it. Tammy wanted no part of it. Mary was freaked out. She'd already had her own paranormal experiences and had not adapted to them very well. Tammy and Mary tried to communicate more with the spirits and said the planchette was moving. I didn't believe any of it. And besides, I was engrossed in a magazine I shouldn't have been looking at. I absentmindedly suggested the bible again and started playing the organ while flipping through the magazine.

And then it got real.

Tammy's little dog started barking out the front window. We looked out, expecting her parents to walk in anytime. (I flung the magazine back onto the top of the refrigerator.)

And the dog kept barking.

We heard something in the backyard and peeked out the vertical blinds, not seeing anything. The dog ran into the dining room and barked at the blinds. We saw a shadow walk across the patio.

And the dog kept barking and went back to the front of the house. We shut out the lights and peeked out the front. Tammy made sure the doors were locked. We were all scared.

Finally, Tammy put her dog in the basement, where she kept barking.

We thought this was a good time to put the Ouija board away and threw it in the box. Armed with steak knives, we walked down the extremely dark hallway to Tammy's room, shoulder to shoulder.

Tammy opened the door.

The room was dark.

All of us distinctly heard a hissing noise like a snake in the room. We all gasped.

Tammy threw the game in the room closing the door.

We ran back to the living room where we tried to analyze everything. We thought briefly of calling my parents but we knew that would mean that we would never be able to come back.

The dog was *still* barking.

We sat in the living room until her parents came home, steak knives in hand. No one tried to get in that we know of. Nothing was out of place outside. We tried to impress upon her parents the events of the evening (minus the magazine), but I don't think they believed us.

Eventually we had to go to bed. When we went back to her room, feeling somewhat safe now that Tammy's parents were home, we looked behind the door and there was nothing, absolutely nothing that could have made that noise. No pom-poms. No door brushing on carpet. Nothing.

That evening, we spend an uneasy sleep in that room. The next day, I remember being insanely tired and happy to fall asleep that afternoon in my own house where I knew what the ghosts were up to (or so I thought).

That night, however, it was all about the Eagles. It started with folks telling us that the cleaning lady hears someone calling her name. Some people told us that they hear "things" or tables moving around upstairs when no one is around. Karen said "nostalgia" comes to mind when she look into the ballroom. She could picture "the women in gowns and the dancing, and oh, God what this once was." True, the building was showing its age and the upstairs is no longer used, but the bones are absolutely beautiful. Karen went on to say that she'd love to do a camp out upstairs, but has yet to find any takers- or gain permission.

At one time, Karen went to the upstairs with a medium, but she wasn't "impressed," especially when he "shot through the bar." When asked what was wrong, he told her, "I stepped three steps off the elevator and all at once it was like someone got me by the cheek of my ass and did like that." Karen motioned as though someone was pinching a butt cheek. She said that there was an older lady up there who liked to pinch butts, but she didn't say if she was living or dead.

Karen went on to tell me about living in a house where a CB enthusiast had lived. Every now and then, they'd hear a CB radio in the house. They believed it was the gentleman who died talking on his radio. Before he died, he was bed bound and his only enjoyable activity was talking with the outside world on his CB. "Every now and then we'd hear a radio playing." She would open the door to his room and it would stop. Close it and the talking would start again.

About that time, Bob Everett arrived. He sat down and ordered a drink. Everyone was talking amongst themselves and for me; it was good to see the homey feel in the room. Bob was part of the reason we were there. I'd contacted him through a friend and only realized when he arrived that he had been my neighbor for 12 years when I lived near Lapel. He told us that he personally had seen his saw kick on "and (it) hasn't done that since." He is a true believer in ghosts "after what I heard about the family home of my wife, Sharon."

Apparently, a grandson in the family was not well liked by his grandmother. She went so far as to say Mike, the grandson, would never inherit the house. When the grandmother died, through divvying up the estate, Mike did receive the house. He lived in it for a while. He witnessed things fly off the mantle. Doors flew open at all hours and finally, he got to sleeping outside the house, on the property in his truck. Even Mike's girlfriends wouldn't stay for more than a night or two. Finally, Mike gave up and said, "I won't go in that house again."

Sharon even told us that she heard her name called in the bar area. She isn't afraid. It is what it is to her.

Tom, Peg, Tammy, Michael, and I decided to go upstairs. The elevator was not modern per se. It was a Warner "Electric" elevator. It functioned, but didn't quite stop right on the floor it was aiming for. We stepped off and the first thing that struck me was the wonderful Art Deco stair railings. You just don't see stair railings like these except in old department stores and converted bank buildings from the 1940s. These were painted gun metal gray with simple craft lines with a clean machine age medallion on each panel. Other areas of the building were a mix of plaster, converted 60s lighting and an industrial look due to disuse. Many rooms were used for storage and you could see the layers of the decades in each room.

We walked up the short flight stairs and got a glimpse of the ballroom. I understood what Karen was talking about. The ballroom was gorgeous, even in its state of disrepair. Parts of it were a mishmash of styles, but the beauty was not dimmed. The ceiling was at least 20 feet tall and beams ran the length of the space. At the end of each beam was an Art Nouveau motif. The windows were all privacy glass blocks but the diffused sunlight still streamed in. Between each window was a small wall sconce, used to create indirect lighting during performances. To the right was a large curved stage with a baby grand piano sat in the middle of the stage, with large drapes framing it.

The gorgeous stair rails!

The stage itself had seen better days. The paint was peeling, the wooden floor was peeling but I could still see the beauty in the simplicity of the space. The bowed front of the stage was also Art Deco with a keyhole motif. The back of the stage had a grand eagle and "174" painted on it.

Above, the beautiful remnants of the stage, complete with piano. Below, the lights are right even if the bulbs aren't!

Looking to the back of the large space (it had to be every bit of 60-80 feet to the back of the ballroom), I looked up to see several large chandeliers. Each chandelier appeared to be bronze or iron and have two layers of lights suspended by heavy chains. Eagles surrounded the circles of lights. A multitude of light would have come from the 10+ bulbs on each light. A bit of water damaged marred the ceiling.

The floor was tiled, with a few patches pulled up. The very back of the space had a balcony, which revealed several rooms behind it. Under the balcony was an unused restroom and a doorway that lead to a storage area under the balcony.

This space amazed me. Almost 100 years of Eagles history was in this spot. Band uniforms, instruments, awards, records and pictures. Old beverage bottles, dance notices, costumes, coat racks and many other items were stored here. The whole area was a time capsule and I was grateful to be able to look through it.

We were waiting for one more person, and while we marveled and waited, Tom Ferguson told us once while Bob was playing the piano, the sounds of dishes and glass breaking happened after he stopped. Neither man could explain the noise.

A few minutes later, Dixie Kirkwood, one of the other FOE members, joined us. Around the organization, she is the one who notices most of the action- or at least she's the most vocal. Dixie was a delight. I am not sure if she knew what to do with Michael and I at first, and she told her story in pieces. Dixie explains, "I feel presences." There is a ghost named Anna that was up on stage as we spoke. Dixie said that Anna stays mainly upstairs, but that sometimes she comes downstairs. Another ghost, Constance, is upstairs, which is where she stays. A third spirit, Horace, was in the building "because he wants to be."

Before the Eagles building was built, there was a house on the site. Dixie feels Horace belongs to the building and he is from the 1940-1950s. Horace always "bows his head." I was unable to find proof of this in land records, but the courthouse had a few devastating fires, so this information could be lost.

Anna and Constance are almost always together and go back "further than this building." Dixie feels they are from the late 1700s to early 1800s, but that they show themselves as is they've been through different time periods and choose to show themselves in the early 1900s style with "old hair". Anna speaks for all and is younger than Constance. The stage and piano is Anna's special area. When I asked if there was anything Anna wanted to tell us, Dixie said, "She said, 'Damn no!'"

Dixie went on to say, "I feel things and that's what I do. I don't get help or training. I am scared of those places. I am not sure why, but I am. I have a spirit guide."

We felt a male presence in the rooms behind the balcony. We went to investigate. At first, the spirit was curious. Dixie told us the spirits move items in the building. She stated, "I am not afraid of spirits but it is a spooky room. I feel the joy has been stripped out and this is all that is left."

Dixie finally told me that she knew she had a gift when she was three or four years old. Her house shook and a bird hit the house. When her grandmother finished explaining the meaning, Dixie said, "I hid it for years. Then I thought, 'I'm 68 years old, who cares? My kids knew about it long before I told them."

Dixie also believes her father had the gift too. When he was dying, he told Dixie that basically he wasn't going to last long and "grandma and grandpa are always with me." Then she turned to me and told me that someone followed Tom to the balcony.

The air was full of what I can only describe as electricity. Anna still wasn't talking. I was getting a semi-hostile vibe and thought she didn't like me. I explained to the spirits what I was doing and that I was not there to change anything or to take their spaces. Dixie said, "These aren't mean ones," meaning Anna, Constance and Horace were not mean. "They've rocked my chair on the ground floor."

Dixie and I compared notes on the idea of being interested in the paranormal or having gifts. She admitted in the past, she had problems with people having issues with what she does. But she doesn't care anymore. I can relate. Michael and I have been called Satan worshipers, anti-Christ, anti-Jesus, etc. None of which is true. Michael is Jewish and I am no religion. I don't worship anything. We've also had people spontaneously try to "bless" us. You can imagine how that turned out!

At that point, Forrester, Dixie's spirit guide, told her to back off from the trio of spirits.

I still felt an antagonistic presence. Dixie said Anna didn't have an issue with me "per se" but this place is hers. Out of the depths of the room, Peg said, "Well she needs to clean it up!"

The balcony area was beautiful with full on windows shining lights into the dressing rooms. A series of rooms connected to each

The balcony and the area in which we saw and spoke to Joel.

Left, the hallway in which we saw Joel.

other but with their own doors spanned the space. Rich dark wood doors, frames and chairs proved this space was once very loved.

As we walked the area, Dixie said she didn't like the man in the hallway. I had seen a dark shape at the end of the hallway that ducked into the last room. I offered the spirit a chance to identify through my digital voice recorder. It didn't respond.

Once in the room the spirit went into, Dixie said it "didn't feel right". I felt a heavy presence as well. Dixie thought he said "jolly". I sat in the balcony to try to avoid the heavy feeling. It was not good for me.

Dixie called out and said she" got corrected." The word was "Joel", not "jolly". I immediately thought of "Joely" as some men named Joel are nicknamed, but she didn't think that was what he said. Joel told her he had acreage on the property. Dixie said he was asking her to leave (for an unknown reason).

We left the balcony and headed back downstairs. Dixie said Anna was on stage and she was in a better mood. I saw a young woman very briefly. She was about 17 and short in early 1900s clothing. When I described this to Dixie, she said this was not Anna or Constance.

One of the Eagles members was playing the piano quite beautifully when we returned to the ballroom. I approached the stage via the left stage door. I was somewhat drawn to this area. Even with the water damage and broken plaster, the dust and god knows what else, the piano sounded absolutely beautiful. Someone touched my arm as I came through the stage left door. It felt like someone running a finger up it and it felt like a spider web attaching itself to my arm. When I returned home and replayed the recorder later, at the same time I was touched, a whistling "wooooooooo" came through the area. It was nice to be acknowledged by Anna.

The lady playing the piano said her daughter had "the gift" and told us when her daughter was 3 years old, she said, "Jenny's with me." After a little research, the FOE member said that the couple a few doors down from them lost their child. A while later, her daughter said, "Jenny's gone. She went home ."

Once we'd gathered everyone, we moved on to the basement. Tom, Michael and I took the elevator down to the basement. The basement was used as a bingo and entertainment room. People can rent the area for a fee and have the use of the room, kitchen and bar. Tom

The basement in which Tom and Bob heard the saw turn on.

told us some of the men who used to clean the building "years ago" also heard things. He showed us the area and told us, "When Bob and I were changing out the furnace, we heard hammering. I don't know what the guy was trying to help us with, but we heard it." Around the same time, Bob heard his saw kick on and he simply shut it off.

I find this information so interesting. Generally, women are all about asking the how and whys of a haunting. Men either accept it and move on or deal with whatever needs to be dealt with and don't talk about it. I love the way Bob and Tom are so nonplussed about their experiences.

Some explanations for the hauntings may go beyond former members or people who owned the property. For decades, the FOE members were told that there are tunnels somewhere in the building that date to the Underground Railroad that were later used for gamblers. Unfortunately, a man named Tucker, Tom told us, who passed away, could have been a great resource.

Apparently Anderson had its share of rough folks. Tucker asked Tom one day if he noticed the way Dick, the old and now deceased owner of Eastside Lanes, walked. Tom said, "Sure, I do." Tucker told him that Dick "had gone down" an elevator shaft because he wasn't "paying" quickly enough and "they made a believer out of him."

Tom chuckled and said, "Whether that is true or not, I cannot say but it was haunted out there."

He went on to say that Mike, who ran the Pro Shop, was changing some paneling. Mike believed that Pappy Carr, who used to bowl and work there, got mad and knocked it over. He said, "Ok Pappy, damn it. Go sit down someplace!"

The Eagles made us feel so welcome. A couple showed us the women's meeting room in which some of the original lights of the State Theater reside. They talked about what a good organization and what good people belong to it and invited us back. Talking with them made me wish for the time that they came from. In their day, people were much more caring, in my opinion. People care today too, but with the rush and bustle of life, sometimes that sort of thing gets overlooked.

Bob says that the FOE is "people helping people." They raise money for Riley and Peyton Manning Hospitals, among other things. Recently, the Eagles made a commitment to raise $25 million to fund a diabetes center at the University of Iowa. "Eagles don't brag. We do a lot of good, but we don't brag."

I've always said everyone has a story of something they can't explain. Whether in the Eagles building or their personal lives, the members of the FOE certainly have lived interesting lives. The FOE is a great organization. A place of beauty, friendship and caring, it is no wonder why ghosts want to stay with them.

St. Mary's School and Church
1115 Pearl Street, Anderson, Indiana

In the early days of Anderson, Delaware (Lenape) and Miami Indians made their homes throughout the territory. Because of the Treaty of St. Marys (Ohio), the Native Americans had to abandon their lands. The treaty was signed by Chiefs William Anderson (Kikthaweund), John Killbuck (Gelelemend), James Nanticoke (meaning "tide water people"), Captain White Eyes (Coquethagechton/Koquethagechton-chief of the Turtle tribe of Delaware) and others. Chief White Eyes' land was later used as the county poor farm.

The City of Anderson was named for Captain Anderson because his village was here. It was a log cabin he shared with his son-- where the Madison County jail stands. He picked this spot because it was beautiful and there was an abundance of water. At the time, he could see over the entire area of what is now downtown Anderson. From what is now W. 7th Street, bounded by the White River and Meridian Street south of Pearl Street, the Lenape used the land. Killbuck also had a village near the creek (SW of CR 75 and CR 300N). Nanticoke had one named Nancy Town (Nancytown, Nantico, Nantikoke) (where Forkner's book states there is an Indian burial ground and where it was once known as McClintock) and it was located on the south side of 800W and Eighth Street. "Our Town", the second known village is believed to be at 400W and Eight Street.

At one point, John Conner, grandson of Chief Anderson, came to Andersontown as it was known them, dressed as a Native American and had a meeting his grandfather and other important Native Americans in the Long House or the Council House, on the site where St. Mary's Catholic Church now sits. Because he was well acquainted with the Native American ways and was strongly built, people couldn't tell he was a white man. John and Chief Anderson smoked a pipe and chatted.

The area around St Mary's has seen several cemeteries. The first cemetery was called Bolivar or the City Cemetery. It was on Bolivar Street (now 10th street on the east side of Fletcher Street). According to Forkner's history, this was also the site of a Delaware Native American burial ground. When the Pittsburg, Chicago and St. Louis Railroad came through, the cemetery was moved to the Tharp (sometimes Thorpe) Cemetery at Eleventh and Delaware Streets. Eventually Tharp Cemetery was moved to a new Cemetery called West Maplewood Cemetery.

The cemetery was to the area to the north and east of St. Mary's parking lot. When the cemetery was removed make way for the railroad,. some bodies were just pushed into the gravel and dirt used to build up the railroad tracks. Soon, squatters and their small homes filled up the area. Locals called it "Happy Hollow" for unknown reasons (perhaps because the people were happy they paid no taxes!) and others called it "No Man's Land" because no one living there had title to the land. They were indulged by the railroad and by the people who lived around them.

The area of St. Mary's today, stretches from Pearl Street to Fletcher Street and from the alley north of Eleventh Street behind the church to Twelfth Street. In that area, the corner of Twelfth and Pearl Streets is private housing. But this land has some interesting history of its own.

Johanna O'Connor, an old lady, was living with her deaf and mute sister in a house on the east side of Pearl Street (the house no longer stands). She had a small orphan girl named Hannah Dunn who did household chores for her. On August 3, 1877, O'Connor told Hannah to light a fire in the stove. Hannah picked up an oil can and poured it on the wood in the stove. Apparently there were some burning embers left in the stove. A flash fire ignited, catching the streaming liquid on fire, exploding the can and setting Hannah ablaze. She "burned to a crisp" in a matter of an "instant."

O'Connor saved her house but did or could do nothing to help Hannah. Witnesses remember hearing the girl cry and scream for a few seconds before her voice was silenced forever. Little Hannah was buried in the Catholic Cemetery south of the city.

Additionally, a house on the north west corner of Pearl and Eleventh Streets (razed) was also reported as haunted. Martha (Baker) Green remembers her grandmother's house. "The house always had an eerie, uncomfortable feel to it as far back as I can remember. I was coming down the stairs when I was about 4-5 years old and was pushed down. My brothers were at the foot of the stairs- there was no one behind me. It had a creepy basement, and the dining room table would periodically make a loud 'crack' sound as if someone were slamming a fist on it. My cousin actually lived there for some time."

Her cousin wrote,

"There were many incidences in that house. There were good spirits and there were evil spirits. It was my job, as early as I can remember, to go upstairs every night before bed to close all the doors. Every night I dreaded that time, absolutely dreaded it. The middle upstairs room directly across from the stairs was where the evil spirits resided. As soon as I would shut all the doors, I immediately had to grab on to the stair railing before I stepped down the first step because they would literally push me down the stairs, and not just a soft push, a hard shove. The first few times I would tumble down several steps. Then I got smart and began running up, close the doors, grab the rail with both hands and run as fast as I could down the steps.

Not only was the house haunted, but there were several male ghosts that would appear to me in the back yard, in the alley behind St. Mary's and in our neighbors yards. The weird thing is, after a tragedy in my family, I was adopted at 13 and did not talk to my biological family for 25 years. I had no clue that they experienced anything in the house, and I never spoke of it to anyone. However, on one of our visits, Martha began to talk about her experiences and other family's stories about things in that house, and I realized that I was not crazy, that it was haunted, and that the evil spirits were not only after me, but anyone who dared venture close to that room at night. In the day the room was ice cold, no matter the time of year, but the spirits laid quiet, but once night fell, that was a whole different story!"

Additionally, another house across the street was supposed to be home to thieves at one time who had hidden gold in it. Although the thieves were never seen, nor the gold, a little boy haunted the house. A gentleman who lived there used to say, "Who's that walking in my house?" Visitors remember seeing the apparition of little boy.

Before the location contained a church, Fathers Francois and Bacquelin came from Logansport to celebrate traveling masses. When they arrived, the first mass (and probably many others) were held in a tavern at the corner of Water and Washington Streets (now 9th and Fletcher)*, at the location of the old Tunnel Bar and on the old Thorp/ Tharpe burial grounds (west side of 12th and Brown-Delaware). Fathers Force and Hamilton continued this work later.

This is an aerial shot of the area around St. Marys. The border of St. Mary's property is in white. Across from the church to the south is a parking lot where the Junior High School was built. The picture shows the old rectory behind that parking lot. In front of the school, the very last house in front of it to the east is the house in which Martha and her family had so many occurrences. The houses are no longer there and the land is part of the church parking lot. The house where the treasure was supposedly hid is across the street from the haunted house. (Photo courtesy of the Anderson Public Library)

St. Mary's Catholic Church & School, Anderson, Ind.

In this postcard, you can see the current church and to the right is the old church, turned school, then razed for a parking lot. It is the location of the old Junior High building. (Photo courtesy of the Anderson Public Library)

From 1840-1858 Fathers Geogham, Murphy, Maloney and Doyal came from Indianapolis and Vincennes to conduct mass in this area and in the Quinlan settlement. In 1858 Father Michael Clarke from Lafayette laid the foundation for the first church, first used as a schoolhouse as well. This was at the northeast corners of Williams and Fletcher streets The citizens donated the money for it and in 1864 the church was built. In 1875 a one-storey rectory was built. In 1873, the southeast corner of Willams and Fletcher was purchased for $1000 and a new church was built. Two years later it was dedicated by the Reverend Bishop Dwenger. In 1893 the current church was built and on October 6,1895 Bishop Joseph Rademacher dedicated it. The old church at the south east corner of Fletcher Street was made into a school. Some of the first teachers were Margaret Moon, Mollie Geisinger and John Finley. The Sisters of the Holy Cross were in charge of the children. Including Sister Victoria O'Keefe.

The 1920s part of St. Mary's. The school is still used for students today.

Some notable highlights in the history of the congregation include:

- 1890 The Fleece family is first African American family in the parish.
- 1920s a new school is needed but they are hesitant to build one because of a law in Oregon that disbanded all Catholic schools and an increased KKK presence.
- 1923-24 This year is the first year for high school course offerings.
- 1964 The junior high (school annex) was built (one storey concrete block building on the location of the first church).
- 1966 Mother Verda Clare tells Monsignor Kienly that the sisters needed to leave and the high school closed. The parish could not afford to pay a completely lay person staff.
- 1974-75 This is the first year all teachers are lay people.
- 2008 All rooms are now air conditioned.

The school was in two parts. The "old part" which was build in the early 1900s and the "new part" that was built later in 1954-55. Additionally, a small cinder block building that served as the junior high sat to the west of the old building. To the southeast was the nun's house, later used for the business office and the priests.

To the back of the buildings was a parking lot/playground and

Nuns taught at the school until 1966. Left, Sister Amanda. Right, Sister Ivan. (Photos courtesy of the Anderson Public Library)

next to it on the west side just north of the alley, was a beautiful house used for the priests.

It is a shame that with all the growth in my area of Indiana and the new(ish) Guerin High School, that St. Mary's couldn't resurrect its high school as well. I was at the school post-nuns and always heard about how mean and strict they were. My own dealing with nuns later in my teens showed them to be strict but not necessarily mean. However, I grew up in a different time.

In my interview with Mary Ann Nivens, the religious director, she told me of her time at the school and her family. I went to school with her daughter, Christy, who was a grade behind me. Mrs. Nivens was very open-minded and helpful during the interview and I thoroughly enjoyed her candor. Her father was one of the first to graduate from the high school. She had an extraordinary amount of stories based on the time the nuns were still at the school. Sisters Aquanada, Adalaide, Alberta Marie, and Amanda to name a few. Search as I might, I did not find many of the nuns she spoke about in the yearbooks (which were admittedly spotty). One comment she made stuck with me. Today, she said, teachers think if the kids are noisy but good, then they are well disciplined. But not in her day.

Mrs. Nivens said they used to go to church often when she was in school and girls will be girls. They used to move each other's purses when they were kneeling in church. It was done in harmless fun, but one girl (you know, "that girl"), decided to tell the nuns that her purse was "gone through" by one of the other girls.

The result was nothing short of a reinforcement of every nun stereotype. Sister Francine took several of the suspected offenders into what is now the uniform cupboard (art supply room in my day), and asked each of them who did it. One unfortunate girl started to nervously smile which got her a slap (as they all got) and the comment, "Who do you think you are, Cheshire Cat?" This was the same nun that told the girls holding hands with a boy was a mortal sin (and punishable by going directly to hell).

Another story was about Sister Ivan. She taught religion and handed Mrs. Nivens' class back a graded test. Next to her desk was a jar of water. Sister Ivan stated, "This jar is for the tears I shed while grading your papers."

Additionally, Sister Miguel taught Mrs. Nivens' father, herself and her brother. Her brother was always a gem in her eyes. But not Mrs.

Nivens, who got the proverbial ruler on the hand on occasion. Even after Sister Miguel retired and Mrs. Nivens wrote to her, she would write back, correcting all Mrs. Nivens' errors on the letter and sending it back.

But not all the stories were bad for Mrs. Nivens. Her brother got some of the brunt too, despite his straight A status. Sister Amanda, an English teacher at the school, used to ask Mrs. Nivens' brother to go shopping for her because she hated going downtown (which was only

Left, the current rectory, formerly the nun's home. Right, the side view of the 1920s school. In the spot where all the rumors stem from, you can see it was a tree garden at this time. But for what purpose? (Photo courtesy of the Anderson Public Library)

about 3 blocks away). Her brother hated it when she asked him to pick up negligees and corsets.

My own sister, Lorri, remembers Sister Alphonsus. She was allowed to stay behind to care for her father after the other nuns left in the 1960s. Mrs. Nivens said she had a sense of humor, which may factor into some of the legends. Lorri remembers helping clean up the rectory and going upstairs to the attic and seeing an enormous brass bed. Sister Alphonsus (who was supposedly a little drunk) said it was "where they kept the bad nuns." The fun part is that after the nuns' home was converted to the rectory, some of the brass beds survived and are still there to this day.

The grassy plot of land, now used as a shady respite for students on a warm day, used to be a flat, treeless spot. In the late 1980s, Gars Nursery used to donate Christmas Trees that were planted after the holidays to beautify this spot. Growing up, the legend was that there was a cemetery in the spot or that the urns at the corner contained babies, the nuns' babies. Or that the whole area was part of a satanic ritual site. After one particularly vocal discussion, the urn disappeared. What an imagination we all had! In reality, this plot was a garden for the nuns. It is unclear whether it was just a formal garden or also a vegetable garden and no known pictures exist of it.

With so much creepy-good history it is no wonder this location has a load of ghosts to go with it. I remember as a child being hesitant to go into some of the bottom parts of the school around the old showers and the boiler room. As I got older, I disliked the back of the gym, and the third floor on the east side- especially when the shadows of the day got longer and less light came in the building. I spend from around 7:00 am to 3:30 pm or longer in the building. My mom dropped me off at school. At various times of year we would either play on the parking lot with tether balls or sit on the wide gleaming wood and tile steps of the "old part" of the school. In junior high, I was on basketball and volleyball teams and usually went to see the boys' teams play.

In fifth grade Lorri had Sister Alphonsus for school. She wrote a report about the French and Indian war including the people and the battle. Sister Alphonsus called her to the desk and she made some comments, but got very particular about how she researched it. Lorri said she made it up, which is true, but she really let herself go into a trance to write it. She got an A on paper.

When Lorri spend time at the rectory, she felt like family. The nuns seemed to get a little "looser lipped" after she'd been around for a while. After she was told about the "bad nuns", she remembered seeing a ghost of a woman in the attic room. She wore a white long nightgown that had border around bottom with ruffle. The top had an empire waist and was high necked. The sleeves disappeared into ruffles at the elbow and she could see through it.

The basement at one time, contained all the records for the church. The floors were hard packed, dry dirt. The walls were brick and stone with door archways made of stone. The rooms went past the side of the house. Some were blocked with wooden doors that went to the school and church. Some of the ceilings were barrel vaults. Some tunnels had flat, high ceilings.

On one occasion when a teenager was helping take some items to the basement, a man came through the door. "It could have been a priest." She was carrying marbles on a box and turned because she heard the click of the door and thought it was a marble. "The figure had a Franciscan brown robe and was an older man similar to Fr. Kienly. He was messing with the door because it had a latch, turned and looked down after he shut the door. It no longer had a handle. It was a great door, curved to fit the arch of the ceiling.

At first, she didn't think anything of it, because he was a priest. His hood was not on his head and he had soft slipper types dark brown or gray shoes. His brown robe ended at the top of his shoe and he had a cloth belt around his waist. The figure turned around and looked at her and back at his hands. She checked her load and back at him and he was gone. Although she was "slightly creeped out", she went back to the basement several times that day and many times afterwards.

The rectory isn't the only creepy place. Longfellow Park (now Longfellow Plaza Senior Community) is home to the ghost of a little boy who died at the park and can be heard crying at night.

The basement of the church, which is the site of the Long Council building where the early Native American's would come to talk about their grievances and come to a consensus on topics, also has a ghost.

Most of the action is centered in the northern section of the basement. As you come down the stairs from the east side of the church you are brought into a large room. To the right is the kitchen and bathrooms. To the left is the large room that is used as the cafeteria. Former members of the staff say that when they used to spend time in the kitchen, it creeped them out. "It was eternally musty and smelled of mold," said one woman.

Bill Smith caught a glimpse of a priest in the area.

"I came down the east stairs to the basement and I saw him in front of me. I called out, but he didn't stop. He turned and went into the kitchen area. I thought it was strange as the lights were off and he was just walking in the dark. I followed and called out, "Father?" but no one answered. I flipped on all the lights looking for him. I heard a huge thump in the back of the kitchen. A mop that had been in a bucket of water, hit the wall." He paused, *"I didn't actually see it hit, but there was a wet spot about 3 feet*

up and the wet mop was under it. The bucket was about 6 feet away. Now how could that have happened? I couldn't believe what I was seeing." Billy shook his head, *"I picked up the mop, put it back in the bucket and noticed that the water was warm. No one was scheduled to be down there cleaning. I was just going down to pick up some papers I left down there. I had to unlock the door to get in!"* Billy finished, *"I checked the other door, which was locked as expected, picked up my papers and left."*

He is not the only one who's seen a figure in the basement. Many people believe that when someone passes, the person can be held on Earth by unfinished business or vibrations of the past can be released. Other people, such as myself, believe that ghosts are transient and can move where ever they want. They don't have to be tied to any area.

Richard said he came face to face with a priest who was in the area in the 1970s. "I read one of the readings at mass and I forgot my bible and other things at the side of the alter. I genuflected at the front of the alter and crossed over to get my things. As I was coming back across the alter, I saw Fr. Fennessy standing in the newer part of the church. I called out to him, surprised because I had not seen him in a good many years. I reached the edge of the new section and hurried over to meet him. I called, "Father Fennessy, how good it is to see you!"

"He turned my way. There was something that didn't look right, but I couldn't put my finger on it. He gave me a vacant stare and walked toward the sacristy. I thought perhaps something was wrong and followed him. But he wasn't there. No one was. I realized what I must

Father Roy Fennessy, circa 1976.

have seen. And looking back on it, I think he was in black and white, and what seemed so unnatural is that his skin was very white against his black clothing. I've never seen him since."

Father Roy T. Fennessy was a priest at St. Mary's for several years. He graduated from Mount Saint Mary (Emmitsburg, Maryland). He was put into rehab for alcohol and possible drug abuse. Later he traveled to several other churches in Indiana. He landed at St. Paul's Catholic Church in the 1980s. I remember when a friend of mine, Nancy Concepcion, went to confession. It was a face to face conversation on a church pew in St. Paul's Church in Marion, Indiana. As they sat there she said she'd cheated on most of his tests. He laughed and asked, "Do you think I'm stupid? I make my tests so hard no one can pass them without cheating!" When he was teaching religion class one day, he tried talking to us about sex. Fr. Fennessy stated, "You can ask me any questions, and I will answer them for you." Tommy, a very tall redhead piped up, "Hey Father, are you a virgin?" The priest smiled and went completely beet red. And never answered the question.

The inside of St. Mary's Church. The doors where the blue figure was seen are in the back under the balcony.

After I left the school, I found out he had been accused of molesting teenage boys. In 1993, he was found dead in his home with a plastic bag tied over his head. It is a horrible situation, especially when he was really good at working with teenagers.

Additionally, both men and women report hearing the doors to the restrooms open and close, when they know no one else is in the basement. "Hearing that leaves you with a pretty unsettled feeling, especially when you hear the footsteps go up the stairs."

The church itself is home to a spirit or two as well. A woman in black sits in the back of the church. She is petite and wears a long black dress, with long black sleeves and gloves. She has a large hat on her head with a veil that hangs on all sides. No one has seen her face. When approached, she disappears. Although her identity is a mystery, people have created a persona for her. She's believed to be the wife of someone who died back in the early 1900s, based on her clothing. Other people believe she tragically lost a child and/or husband and died of a broken heart.

After Sunday mass, the church cleared out and Beth was alone. The priests were either outside greeting people or back in the sacristy. The enormous space seemed "charged with a peaceful energy".

She looked to the back and saw a black figure behind the doors. At first, she thought it was a trick of light but as she looked closer it was a medium height shadow figure. It closed the doors in front of her then moved to the side to close another. The last door was open and the figure moved to it, but instead of closing it, the figure oozed through and came toward Beth.

The school has its own phantom issues. In the same uniform cupboard where Mrs. Nivens was slapped, students and staff see a nun. She is described as wearing a long dark overskirt that stands slightly out (as if it is worn with an underskirt) with a light colored guimpe over the top. She has on a long dark veil with a white underveil. Alternately, some people report seeing a cross about her neck and others report a cross around her waist, such as with a rosary. Dark shoes peak out from under her skirts.

Most people report seeing her and she walks away, sometimes down the hall, sometimes disappearing up the stairs to the uniform cupboard, sometimes just disappearing in place. She sometimes is facing away but at least once, someone has seen her face.

Tracy was coming around the corner of the hall to get into the cupboard. As she turned "a nun came up the stairs." She had on the same habit others saw her in. "As she hit the top stair, before she turned to go up into the cupboard, I said, "Excuse me, Sister. I didn't mean to startle you."

"The nun looked directly at me and said, 'I'm not startled! Now if you'll let me go about my business!" and she turned, went up the stairs and melted into the door."

"I knew what I'd seen. And I was more surprised at the clarity of the voice and the way she looked than by the fact I'd seen a ghost. I looked through some of the yearbooks but never found her picture. She was medium build and middle aged. She had a severe looking nose and dark eyes."

For years, students, teachers and other staff have seen wispy white and black mists and shadows in the showers and bathrooms. In the 1950s section of the school, the Boys locker room is a place where children often see shadow figures. Most times they are seen disappearing into the shower area of the locker room. Ann*, a former student, was shocked when she saw something more. At the time, the locker room was used by girls because it was far more comfortable than their own locker room.

"It wasn't uncommon to feel watched. The girls thought it was our basketball coach or one of the younger custodians. Creepy, but not paranormal. Once, I went back to the locker room to get a ponytail holder. As I opened the door, I could see a reflection on the wall that was directly in front of the door. I peeked in and saw a bright light in the mirror, that seemed to reflect onto the wall.

I didn't know what was going on. I opened the door full on and walked to the edge of the wall. In the mirror and moreover in front of me, I saw a beatific vision of a woman. She was in a habit and the light shining from her was warm and comforting. I believe it was a nun who protected the place. I watched her for a couple of minutes, completely enraptured, and she slowly faded away."

This locker room is right on the edge of the new and old space. It is interesting because going north from the locker room and then east leads you down one of the hands-down creepiest school areas I have ever been in.

As a child, I remember hearing what sounded like basketballs dropped on the floor or the gym when no one was there. I remember taking a "short cut" across the stage to avoid the dark passage (never mind that the stage was usually darker!). Footsteps always seemed to follow one in the hallway.

It didn't help that the girls bathroom was strangely laid out. You would walk in and on the left were the stalls, on the right was a wall and later on the same side, a large mirror. You could turn left and there were the sinks, with another row of toilets. When I was there, the second row had been disabled, but the pipe chase between them could be opened and there were a host of unappetizing things, including toilet paper and used feminine products. Who said girls were cleaner than boys? In the back of the bathroom next to the sinks was a huge opening, which we all speculated was a fireplace (in a bathroom?) but was most likely an air return.

To the east of the bathroom was a girls' locker room. It was a remnant of the 1920s to be sure. It had the same industrial floor, the little shower lips. And a common stall-like layout which let anyone and everyone in the showers view you. I avoided the area whenever possible. There was a door which led to another room to the east. Someone told me that was a mini infirmary at one point. I can't confirm this as the glass was too frosty to see anything inside.

What seems stereotypical today, but which scared the bejeus out of us all was being asked to go to the boiler room. It was loud, dark, and noisy. When sent down there, one could never find the janitor (who was rightfully off doing other things). You could be standing still and you would hear footsteps behind you.

One former student said she went into the music room which is to the west of the girls bathroom, and she saw a black figure in the north east corner of the room. Another former student said that there was a tall, dark figure pacing between the music room and the science lab.

One student was a bit braver. She saw the figure down by the music room and said, "Hey wait a minute!" Running toward the figure, she described it as "kind of scrambling" as if it were surprised someone saw it. She saw it duck around the corner. When she got there, she didn't see it in the hall and decided it must have gone into the gym. She ran up the stairs and stopped short the gym. The east doors were open, allowing some light in. She saw the figure running toward the back,

The hallway where the nun is seen. The uniform cupboard is at the top of the stairs on the right side.

"arms flailing about."

We don't know who most of these spirits are. They could be nuns, students and parishioners from the past. They might also be other spirits brought in, attached to others. Or they could go further back into the time of the Native Americans. In any case, they continue to appear and sometimes delight the people who roam the halls of St. Mary's.

.*This is now gone. It is part of the Madison Co. Job Source and parking lot.

The hallway in the basement where figures are seen walking and in rooms. The girl's restroom is on the upper left and next to it is the creepy old girl's locker room.

The Tunnel Bar, circa 1950. This is the site where some early masses were held before a church was built. It is highly unlikely that the masses were held in this building, but rather in a structure that was here before this building. The Tunnel Bar burned in the 1970s. It had an interesting history as a rough place with lots of fights, prompting police action. It was owned by Deloris (Turner) Gaw. It was named the Tunnel Bar because of the tunnel under the train track (right side). Notice Norton Brewery in the upper left at the highest point in the photo. (Photo courtesy of the Madison County Historical Society)

Camp Chesterfield
North of SR32 on Washington St., Chesterfield, Indiana

In 1843, Dr. John Westerfield advocated speakers in the meta-physical area. Attracting speakers from all areas of life, these popular events were held at the Union Hall in Anderson. Billed as "scientific investigation societies" attendees were treated to talks about clairvoy-ance, spirit speaking, phrenology, trances, and numerous other spiritu-al areas.   Groups around the country converged to form the Mod-ern American Spiritualism movement, including the Indiana Association of Spiritualists. In 1855 Dr. Westerfield and his wife lost their 14 year old son John Jr. They tried a medium to talk to him after his passing.

For Spiritualists, séances and other metaphysical events be-came a part of daily life. The Quakers shared John's views during the Civil War years and helped him with work on the Underground Rail-road. On what would become Camp Chesterfield, a tunnel leading to a woodpile exit was created. After a visit to a spiritualist camp in Michigan during 1883, Dr. Westerfield came back an established what is now Camp Chesterfield.

Carroll and Emily Bronnenberg sold 30 acres of land to the camp. They and their family were amply involved in the spiritualist movement. They built an Italianate home over the tunnel that was con-nected to the original Bronnenberg farm barn, which was razed. A large auditorium for 500 people and houses for mediums were built. A yearly meeting was held in August to revive their "peculiar faith" according to Forkner.

Over the years, many people have claimed the camp or at least the followers are tricksters, performing hoaxes for paying visitors. In the early 1900s, Houdini himself denounced the camp, citing some of his own magician's tricks as being employed on the premises. In 1925 a reporter filed charges stating the people at the camp were obtain-ing money on false pretenses. Throughout much of the 1900s, others came forward and denounced the camp. Others perpetrated hoaxes and later came clean about them.

Madam Mimi was one of the earliest debunkings. After seeing her show, a reporter wanted to do a story on what he'd seen. His editor suggested they return– with magicians. Once they'd seen the show, the magicians deemed it all fake. They set up an appointment with Madam

Mimi and gave her a dose of her own medicine. They used her same tricks and then some on her. She was reported as saying that she didn't know "what the hell" was going on but that it "wasn't part of the act" and she made a hasty retreat.

One of the more well known debunkings came in 1977 when former camp minister Lamar Keene came out with a book and interviews on the types of hoaxes perpetrated. He also said there is a secret vault under the chapel that houses records on frequent spiritualists. These are shared across the globe for spiritualists to use in "hot readings," which is used in a group situation. In 2002 Joe Nickell debunked the location even further by posing as a person reeling from the death of his mother. The mediums said they had contact with her. In reality his mother was quite alive and well.

Still, many people believe this peaceful, spiritual place is full of hauntings. And why wouldn't it be– especially with all the psychics and mediums around. Michael and I have been to Camp Chesterfield many times. It is always a quiet, serene place. We tend to go when no one seems to be around, but we have seen a few heads peeking out of windows.

When we visit, the Sunflower Hotel to the left of the entrance is enchanting in it's historic simplicity. Sporting a wide two story veranda, one can imagine people taking respite from the heat under the protective canopy of wood and paint.

The Sunflower Hotel. Still beautiful after all these years.

The newer visitor's center welcomes people from far and wide. For years, people have come from all over the US and the world to visit this unassuming place. The grotto which has a statue of Jesus said to move his hands, and Budda (aka Gnome) garden which contains busts of some of the earliest spiritualists continue to attract people seeking solace and answers. In the far back of the main grounds, is a totem where spirit guides come to recharge and to find their intended person. The homes that surround the camp are small, modest looking buildings. Skeptics believe the modesty belies the "exorbitant" amount raked in from camp and spiritualist events. Each home has a sign stating who they are and in what they specialize.

Above, an undated picture of Carroll Bronnenberg. (Photo courtesy of the Madison County Historical Society)

Left, one of the Native American symbols in the camp used as a place of reflection and prayer.

The camp museum has several paintings dating back to the time of John Westerfield and the Fox sisters. They would talk with the spirits, and the spirits would form on canvas through a fine powder of dust, according to some people.

People who live at the camp year round believe ghostly figures roam the ground. One particular favorite is the spirit of Mary. She is supposed to have been the small daughter of Frederick Bronnenberg and is buried nearby.

A small child supposedly haunts the woods near the river. He is seen running through the area in 1940s bib shorts and hard soled shoes with white socks. Both the Western and Sunflower Hotels have reported activity. People hear footsteps and conversation when no one is present.

One group of people who decided to plan a trip had a terrifying dream the night before. All of them dreamed that spirits from the camp were hovering over them and wanted to take them with them. Needless to say, they never went.

The most significant story told to me about this seemingly serene area with a troubled history was from a woman who spent the night at the camp. Her dream came true.

Connie and her friend Jasmine spent the night in the Western Hotel. In the morning, they enjoyed a billet reading and spirit guide ritual in the wooded area behind the visitor's center. They were looking forward to the next day when they were to tour the museum, have private readings and look around the area.

The Western Hotel. A place to sleep well, or watch for spirits?

Their joy was cut short.

That evening, they both went to sleep. Connie woke up in a panicked sweat. She had a dream they were in the grotto and something dark appeared to her. It was not that the figure itself was terrifying; it was more what it represented was terrifying. Connie couldn't explain it and she was tired. She closed her eyes and went back to sleep.

The next morning was bright and clear. They ate some breakfast at a local place and walked the short distance back. Once on the grounds, Connie noticed that despite sun and great weather, a pall seemed to hang over the area. As the pair rounded the curve to go back to their rooms, Jasmine said, "We need to get back to our rooms." She paused, "Now."

Connie felt uneasy as well. She couldn't explain why but they walked more quickly to their rooms. Shortly after they arrived, Connie heard a tapping on her door. Reluctantly, she opened the door.

A woman stood outside. Connie recognized her from the night before. She said as if in a trance, "You need to leave here. Today. Immediately," and with that, she walked away.

Connie ran to her friend's room and told her what happened. Jasmine tried to laugh it off, but she was shaken. "Let's go outside to the grotto."

Connie followed her outside, but the uneasy feeling remained. They walked to the grotto with a couple candles. As they neared, a gentleman exited the area. The pair of women nodded as they passed.

They went inside and lit the candles, sitting on the stone seats. Suddenly, from the side room came a noxious black entity. The smell was as strong as rotten eggs and rotting food.

Connie said, "We need to leave…"

Jasmine finished, "…before he comes!"

The women ran from the grotto, prayer forgotten. They went back to their rooms and hastily packed, chattering about the dream they had. The night before, they both had a nightmare. Both women dreamed they were at the camp with several people who were there for a psychic fair. They went to the grotto where they were alone. As they lit candles to pray, a black mist came from the smaller chamber of the grotto.

At this point in the dream, Connie left, leaving Jasmine alone. Jasmine remembers seeing the mist morph into a noxious smelling beast with long, sharp talon hands. It had no definitive feet, but its face was black and deeply creased, as if scarred. Its sunken red eyes "told the story of ancient evil" and it seemed to "chuckle" as it formed and came towards her. She felt its arms wrap around her and she felt the wetness that seemed to come off it in sheets. Jasmine said she awoke at this point in the dream.

They were "pretty OK" that they had the same dream, however, they were concerned about the content. All they'd ever heard was that Camp Chesterfield was a quiet, peaceful place. That was spoiled for them now.

They had prepaid so they left their keys in the rooms. As they stepped into the hall, They noticed strange, wet footprints that lead to their doors and no one else's. Connie and Jasmine couldn't leave fast enough.

At the grotto.

Elwood Opera House
202 South Anderson Street, Elwood, Indiana

When Gustav V. Kramer emigrated from Fulda Germany in 1835, I highly doubt he knew what a lasting impact he would have on today's society. When he first came over, he lived near Cincinnati. He was a barrel maker (cooper) and earned his money doing just that. "Gus" as he was called, moved to Elwood when he heard that hardwood was plentiful for barrels and casks. He bought a lot of land and opened his stave and barrel factory. He added a lumber yard and an excelsior factory. Later he owned ponds for ice and three ice houses.

As you can imagine, he had some wealth and was one of the most influential builders in Elwood. His children received his estate after his death. Despite his wealth and good fortune, he was kind and humble, giving unreservedly, especially to St. Joseph's Catholic Church.

He built Elwood's first opera house in 1887.* The second and third floors housed the opera house and the bottom floors were businesses. It was located at South A and Anderson Streets. In the 1890s, some of the most famous acts of the day played the Elwood Opera House including Irish comedians Murray and Mack, Robert Downing, Al G. Field, Leslie and White and several others. Everything from Shakespeare to book adaptations played on stage. Later Al G. Field would bring his act "Darkest America" to the venue. Instead of black-faced white actors, he brought black actors to the stage- and with great success. Several other black acts were to follow, including, "Rusco and Holland's Original Nashville Students" combined with "Gideon's Big Minstrel Carnival." Both had equal success.** It has always been a center of the community, hosting meetings, graduations and most recently dances.

The building was sold and retained by the Masons until 1999. Red Skelton and John Wayne were just two of the famous Masons who visited. It was then sold to Randal Hall. With the help of Keith Israel, the great, great grandson of Gus), a complete remodel was done except on the "Blue Room", which was left as the Masons had it with carpet, rounded ceiling and marble finished pillars. It is still open for events, proms and investigations.

With such an interesting history, the hauntings seem a forgone conclusion. One story is of a boy who died in an area that was used as a doctors office. Another story involves a worker who fell through a trap door above the stage and died.

The one area that seems to have more activity than the others is the famous "Blue Room", which is now a dining area. Investigators seem to capture orbs, feel uneasy and detect more spirits here than any other place in the building. And why not? The room is impressive. With a vaulted ceiling and blue lighting, as well as the Boaz and Joachim pillars from the Masonic era, what ghost wouldn't like to tarry in this area.

Jason, an investigator, told me that when he entered the Blue Room, one of the east side doors opened on its own. "I couldn't believe what I was seeing."

Mary walked through the door that had just opened on its own and immediately felt ill. She was an empath and any psychic impressions they wanted to give her usually gave her a hard impact at first. She descended the stairs and became agitated. She could smell a mix of roses and something that smelled of a cleaning product or rubbing alcohol.

The stairway began to swim in front of her eyes. Mary breathed in heavily. She could feel the sweat run down her back and neck. A feeling of panic rose in her until she screamed. In an instant, she was freezing and she saw a white mist come out of her body, tumbling down the stairs. It transformed into a human figure and faded away. Footsteps ran from the area behind her. Mary whirled but found no one there. She gripped the wall tightly. Mary knew she had just witnessed a death.

And so goes a typical ghost hunt at the Elwood Opera House. Visitors are treated not only to this type of activity but also walking though a vortex on the main stairway. People who sense this vortex say there are many spirits in the building, including the murdered person on the stairs, a small boy, a teenage boy and a middle aged woman who is dressed like a show girl.

The stage has its share of problems. The lights turn off and on at will. Investigators have heard a cry for help, although they seem to be alone.

Mary, the same investigator who saw the spirit tumble down the stairs, said that during her visit, as she walked around the building, shadow figures followed her. One was a malevolent force she believes is the murderer.

"I was on the stage and I heard a strangled cry." Suddenly the words, "Help me." Were whispered quite loudly in my left ear."

Her son, Chase, who was near the French doors leading to the balcony, said they creaked open when no one was near them. "Scared me to death."

In the men's restroom, Chase said he was washing his hands when the lights went out. "I was completely freaked out."

The restroom door opened and a shadow figure about six foot tall and outlined in white walked in, past Chase and through the wall. Trying to digest what had just happened, Chase turned, only to be face-to-face with a similar figure. "I don't know if it was the same one coming back to have another look or a second figure. It reached out to me and brushed it's dark hand across my cheek. I could feel the fingers, they were cool to the touch. And as suddenly as he was there, he left. After that, the lights came back on. I didn't waste time leaving."

The owner said he wasn't really "into" the paranormal but "they like me." When he's used dowsing rods and people ask who the ghosts like best, he says, 'They always point to me."

*Kramer built another opera house, The Kramer Grande Opera House just south of the Elwood Opera House but it burned down in 1919.

**This was before the Klan moved in 1910.

St John's Hospital

2015 Jackson Street, Anderson, Indiana

Uncle John Hickey came from County Wicklow in Ireland to Indiana in 1853. He was a businessman who did well for himself. He had a grocery, restaurant, and a farm, where the first natural gas well in Anderson was founded. When his wife, Maria, died in 1893 of pneumonia, John donated the land to the trustees of the St. Mary's Academy for the Sisters of the Holy Cross. This hospital was unique for the time. Anyone regardless of race, creed or social condition was allowed to use it. It was named St. Mary's for a short period and later St. John's Hospital, named so for John Hickey's patron saint. During the last 10 years of Uncle John's life, he lived at the hospital. Before he died, he burned all the notes, bills and mortgages due to him from the hospital.

The original house was used as a hospital within 69 days. Sister Victoria, who had nursed Union troops during the Civil War, was quick to move things along. She and Sister Giovanni worked at the hospital in addition to their work at St. Mary's School. Soon they were joined by Sisters Leoine and Gonzague. In the beginning it was "have bed, will travel". Patients brought their beds and other items during their stay. The first operation was an amputation of the leg of a man.

One year later a 2-storey brick building opened. It was designed to be added onto if necessary and in 1900 another section was added to it.

As with most large institutions, St. John's was chronically short of money. The Sisters of the Holy Cross lived on donations for the hospital. The city gave free light and water. The sisters were the staff, but they later opened a nursing school in 1909, which undoubtedly brought in some income. A new wing was opened in 1915 which increased the hospital debt. With World War I afoot and doctors joining up, it seemed a desperate situation for the hospital. It got worse after the war when doctors redistributed to rival hospitals.

In order to stabilize the hospital, they formed affiliations with the American College of Surgeons and the American Hospital Association in 1921. Additionally, the hospital created a more efficient staff structure. In 1944, the hospital expanded again. In 1965 the 1900 wing was razed.

As a child, I remember in 1980 that the hospital was changed to the Saint John's Medical Center (and later in 1984 the Saint John's Health Corporation). It opened additional locations in Pendleton, Alexandria, a rehab and mental health clinic, a woman's center, the Archway Adult Day Care Center, an Alzheimer's resource center, and a sports medicine center.

An era ended in 1986 when the Sisters of the Holy Cross, who had administered the hospital for 102 years, were replaced by James H. Stephens. Today it is part of St. Vincent's health care system (St. Vincent Anderson Regional Hospital).

During my time as a candy striper, I worked in the newer section of the hospital. The volunteer program, however, was housed in the older part of the hospital. I remember going down a long, dim corridor and into an old room with one high window to shed light into it. The head of the program gave me the rules (which were that if you didn't show up just once without a really good excuse, you were out) and my assignment.

I felt pretty at home in that area as it was built around the same time as St. Mary's School, where I had just graduated 8th grade from. And based on the issues I had at my own house, this was nothing. One morning, when I went in before my shift to let them know I would be unable to be on site in a couple weeks, I walked through the very empty hall. The walls were just as dark, if not more so because of the overcast day. The rooms were largely locked with their doors closed. (Yes, I was nosy!) Only the room I'd interviewed in was open.

I thought I was going nuts when I got to the doorway. I went in, hearing my feet make noise on the over polished wood floors and saw that the entire room was no longer an office, but a filing room. I didn't know who I should talk to, when a petite nun, stepped out from seemingly nowhere.

Somewhat startled, I asked if I should speak with her. The nun stared. I asked again, thinking she might be hard of hearing. Still nothing. I repeated it more loudly, explaining why I needed to speak with someone. The nun continued to stare at me and disappeared. Maybe she didn't want to deal with it. I didn't know what else to do, so I left and came back later.

When I returned, the person I regularly spoke with was in. I told her I'd tried to come earlier. I asked her who the nun was that haunted the area. The woman looked frightened but covered it up and said she didn't know what I was talking about.

Through our tours and my writing, I am fortunate to meet a lot of people. Many people from Anderson work at St. John's as it is still a major employer in the area. Staff at all levels have experiences at the hospital.

Cleaning staff swear they hear footsteps or see patients walking in hallways when no one is on the floor. Barbara was cleaning a semi-occupied floor stopped at the room of a woman who'd been in the hospital an "awfully long time." Cora, the patient, was happy about going home in a few days. They exchanged a few words and Barbara wished her luck. Smiling, Barbara left and completed her rounds.

A few days later, Barbara cleaned the same floor. She went into Cora's room and saw her sitting up. Barbara asked Cora when she would be going home. Cora said, "Any day now," and smiled. Barbara commented, "Well, let's hope for sooner rather than later," and went to her cart outside the door. As she reached down to pick up some supplies, a nurse asked her, "Sooner for what?"

Barbara said, "Miss Cora. She's leaving soon."

The nurses' face "turned white as rice." She slowly said, "Miss Cora?"

Barbara stood up, "Yes, the lady in this room." She motioned to the room behind her.

Another nurse joined them, "Didn't you hear? Miss Cora died yesterday. She had been doing so well, but she had another stroke. And she didn't make it."

Barbara thought this was some sort of bad joke. "Miss Cora is in here," she insisted. Swinging around, she faced the room. The lights were off, the bed was stripped and all was quiet.

Barbara stared at the women in amazement. "It was all I could do." She related the conversation to the nurses, and they all stood around trying to figure it out. In hushed voices, they figured that a piece of Cora stayed behind because of the bond between the women.

This is not the only example of ghostly activity. Nurses often speak of dying patients as "circling the drain." Sometimes the term is used when someone is so close to death but hangs on for someone or something. Some people argue this term is disrespectful, but I disagree. Nursing and for that matter, the medical field is tough. Whether you're around dying patients or simply dealing with patients, it can be rough. Medical professionals find ways to ease the pressure and one way is coming up with a "short order" type lingo of their own.

Writers of all types have captured stories about relatives, shadow figures and other apparitions appearing to patients before death. I like to think these are similar to the way it was depicted in the movie "Ghost" with Patrick Swayze. And while I don't believe in Heaven or Hell per se, I do believe there is an afterlife and you will be held accountable for your earthly (mis)deeds. But what about the smallest of the dying?

Nancy, a pediatric nurse, worked at the hospital many years ago. "Back then, " she said, "we didn't have as many life-saving options as today." One particular case, she remembers quite vividly. "When newborns died, it was a sad day for everyone. Even though we had new life all around us, a child dying affected us all."

A premature baby was born. The mother died from hemorrhaging and the baby was not expected to live much longer. Nancy was in charge of monitoring the child for the rest of the family who had gathered for the baby's final minutes. "The baby's breathing was very shallow and very slow. Her lungs hadn't developed correctly. I went to fetch water and coffee for the family. I no sooner got to the coffee when I heard a baby crying. That wasn't unusual, given the floor, but this baby could barely breathe. And the cry was so loud and forlorn, it made me hurry back."

"The family was trying to sooth the baby, but to no avail. A sudden wind whipped through the room. An apparition of the child's recently departed mother appeared. The woman was completely transparent and just the outline of her in wisps of white could be seen. She was beautiful as she had been in life. Her face was only marred by a frown as she reached down to her child."

Nancy shook her head, "As soon as she put her white hand on the child's chest, she stopped crying and died. The woman scooped the baby into her arms, touched her husband's face, looked lovingly at the family, and disappeared. The family agreed a sense of peace came over them at that moment. It was like they'd been able to say goodbye."

Like Nancy, Judy has seen a lot in the time she's worked at the hospital. She usually works nights and has access to many areas of the hospital. "People ask you all the time about people dying and how it affects you. Sometimes, I don't know what to say. It is hard, but you can't be sentimental because it affects your judgment and how you can do your job. But you have to keep your compassion, still doing what needs to be done."

"That evening, I had a patient who'd gotten sick and needed her bed changed. We were out of sheets, waiting for the laundry to make its rounds. Rather than call them, since it was a slow evening, I said I'd go get some."

"I went down to the laundry area. It was in the lower level of the hospital. At that time of night, it was pretty dark in the area with minimal staff. There was no one in the main laundry office so I picked up a post it and began to write a note about what I took and what floor had it. The area was toasty warm due to all the dryers running. I put the note down and grabbed what I needed. I walked back through the maze of hallways and returned to the elevator. The lights flickered a little, but I didn't think anything of it."

"The doors to the elevator opened and a solid white floating mass. It had no body and the edges were blurry, but it had something of a face. Big pointy teeth gapped out of its mouth and its eyes were only a white area with a light green and yellow matted pupil. Tendrils of white hair clung in clumps to its head. It seemed to snarl; I was completely terrified. Before I could react, it rushed out of the elevator and flew down the hall. As it went, the lights flickered and burst. I didn't wait to find out what happened to it or anyone else. I got in the elevator and went back to my floor."

"I was a cold but sweating nervous wreck. The other nurses wanted to know what happened. I handed the sheets to one of them and told them the story. They were incredulous. Apparently one of the night laundry workers let it slip that he'd experienced something similar. Only the spirit came through the hallway and then into the laundry room, knocking trays, bins and other containers over in the process. The nurse who told us thought he was just trying to scare her. He told her that it happened almost every night at the same time, which is when he took his break."

No one knows what this entity is. The laundry is very close to the morgue and the laundry worker wondered if it was a disgruntled old man who was trapped in the hospital, angry that he was dead, or that he hadn't gone yet.

The hospital was built on thanks for a job well done and continues in the same tradition today. The next time you walk into the lobby, think about what you can't see or what you can that lurks in the different areas.

St. John's in the early 1900s. Notice the original Hickey Farmhouse on the right side by the tree.

Maplewood Cemetery

East: 200 College Drive, Anderson, Indiana
West: Corner of Alexandria Pike and Grand Avenue

West Maplewood Cemetery was founded in 1907. Many citizens of Anderson who owned plots in Anderson Cemetery asked the Maplewood Cemetery Association to care for their cemetery as well so that it would not be abandoned or left to rot. Today a not-for-profit board of trustees care for both West and East Maplewood.

These cemeteries are joined not only by name and proximity but also by the people that reside in them. James Tharp's 1846 Federal period stone represents one of the earliest settlers in the county, People from all walks of life were truly joined in death by their interment in the cemetery. A Titanic survivor, the Remy Brothers, several military personnel, and an early feminist are some of the known people buried in the soft earth. Tharp, the old City Cemetery, and Anderson Cemetery are all part of the Maplewood experience now.

Perhaps the most famous of all the beautiful markers in this cemetery are those of sister and brother. Gertrude's obituary shows she died of diphtheria. Charlie's cause of death is bone erysipelas. He had inflammatory rheumatism. Because of this, he had a leg amputated and died shortly after. Life sized statues of both children mark their resting place. People come from all over central Indiana to place flags and flowers on the stones. Charles leans on a column, symbolizing a noble life and Gertrude's book stands for the divine word.

Their father, Dr. George N. Hilligoss, who was also the founding president of the Indiana Association of Spiritualists, and his wife Caroline, were devastated at the death of their children. They had these Italian marble life-sized statues made for each child by a master sculptor in Florence Italy. He sent letters to the Anderson Herald claiming he when he visited a medium at Terre Haute, his daughter appeared, spoke with him and blew him kisses- in addition to speaking with his mother, brother and a sister that he was previously unaware of. Charlie also witnessed these events. Dr. Hilligoss was ecstatic and felt a sense of comfort from the events.

As a side note, until Camp Chesterfield was functional, the Indiana Association of Spiritualists met in several places, most commonly, private homes and in the building at the NW corder of 13th and Madison Ave.

As one can imagine, there are many stories associated with this cemetery. Between the tragic loss of young life, the new interments from other cemeteries and the people who bought plots in the cemetery, one would be disappointed if there were no stories at all.

For as long as I can remember (and that is a very long time!), the local legend was that the Hilligoss statues would bleed from time to time. Some people said it was on the anniversary of the children's' deaths. Other people said it was when they wanted new accouterments for their memorials.

But that's not all. In the past, I've wondered about people who live across from cemeteries. What do they see? Do they see anything? The people who live near both parts of these cemeteries claim there is more than just a serene setting of an evening. Several people interviewed claimed that white shadows move through the cemetery, drifting from place to place. Other people told me they see orbs in the east and west cemeteries.

One gentleman was driven to drinking. As Sam* stood outside smoking a cigarette, he watched four white figures gliding through East Maplewood cemetery. "At first, it was like they were walking. I though it was just a group of people in light clothing or people pulling a prank. I continued to watch because if they were going to do something harmful, I was going to call the police."

What Sam saw next surprised him. "They were no longer walking or gliding, I saw two of them raise higher than the rest and break away from the pack. The two that were floating went back the way they came and the others continued to move toward the south. I'd had enough and went inside. I kind of stopped looking over that way when I smoked."

Janice was not quite as scared. She saw figures similar to the ones seen by John. But she went after them. "I grabbed my flashlight and headed across the street. I'd always been fascinated by the paranormal. The gates were closed but I shimmied over the fence." As she hurried to catch up with the spirits, they all stopped and moved up, seeming to be aware something was going on outside their realm.

"The group turned towards me and drifted at a good clip toward me. They were about 50 feet away when I got a good look at them. They seemed to be two men and two women. They were white outlines but I could see one man had some sort of striped pattern on his shirt and the women wore long pencil skirts."

"They stared at me with my flashlight and I stared at them looming over me. They passed by me, deliberately going around me, but staying high up. Their feet, or what should have been their feet, were level with my head. They had no feet but just wisps of white. It really looked like clouds. Anyway, they stared at me as they passed and as they moved on, they turned away and continued drifting at the same height back where I saw them come from originally."

Janice said she didn't feel scared, except when they originally approached her. "I remember just feeling this icy energy coming from them. They seemed to be bright as light bulbs but the air around them was cold."

From that time on, Janice saw them often. She tried a few more times to go over to speak with them or at least capture them on camera. However, all pictures came up without their images in them and any time she called out to them, they would "immediately" disappear.

Another story relates to East Maplewood in the 1980s on Thanksgiving morning. Dave, a policeman and his mother are paying respects to his dad, her husband. The ground was covered with snow and it was a bit brisk. They put a wreath on the grave and stayed wrapped in their thoughts.

The policeman's mother says, "Why is that man watching us from behind the tree?"

The policeman looks up and sees a man behind a tree. Although his clothes are more nineteenth century than current, Dave tells his mother they should probably leave.

When they leave, Dave looks in his rear view mirror and sees the figure "running across the tops of headstones, never touching the ground."

Dave takes his mother home and returns. What he finds surprises him. He looks at the area in which he saw the man standing behind the tree. He sees none.

Maplewood Cemetery was established for taking care of the dead and what was left of the human body. It seems the interred inhabitants are amply able of caring for themselves in the afterlife!

The childrens' statues. As beautiful in their sadness as they are heart-breaking in their deaths.

The Travelers
Anderson, Indiana

Before any white man lived on the land that makes up Anderson, it belonged to Native Americans until the 1818 Treaty of St. Mary's. William Conner "helped" Chief Anderson negotiate the treaty, where the Native Americans received some money for the land and its improvements. Still, they were not given a choice about the treaty and were eventually thrown off the land. Soon after the Treaty was official, land grants were given to white settlers who moved onto the land.

George Vineyard was one of those settlers who was given 80 acres in a grant signed by Andrew Jackson on April 1, 1833. He and his family turned the land into one working farm and then later subdivided the property into several working farms. In 1856 the Vineyards gave the railroad rights to cut through their property and therefore usher in a new age. The railroad brought new options to towns in which they operated. Anderson as many other towns in the area, became a hub for industry and trade. The former waterways that were used by traders and Native Americans now gave way to quick transit by railway and later by motorized vehicles.

If you look at the property today, all that is left of George Vineyard's original 80 acre working farm is a barn, a smokehouse, and their pre-Civil War home. The land has been divided, subdivided and now contains homes for hundreds of Anderson citizens. Several homes of George Vineyard's five children still exist on formerly owned Vineyard land. New Jerusalem Gospel Church even has a window dedicated to one of George's brothers, Alvin.

History about the land contained within the city of Anderson is in short supply. In 1910 the courthouse burned to the ground. Citizens were asked to come in and swear affidavit to the effect that they owned the property. They were asked to give any history of their land and asked to bring documents they had regarding their land so the government could recreate these records and store them at the courthouse once again. What we do know about the property is that the land, in addition to having been the Vineyard's farm, the property has always been put to good use.

After George died, his children had their own homes and the house was sold. By this time, because of the proximity to the railroad, some factories were in the area. In those days, homes and factories co-existed with little thought to air quality or toxic waste. Instead of tearing down the house, it was revamped and reinvented for several years.

The home was a multipurpose building throughout its time after the Vineyards owned it. Another family, the Matters, bought the house and briefly stayed there. Why they left abruptly is still a mystery. Next, it was used as a printing house for the Gospel Trumpet and a book-store for Anderson College (now Anderson University). The Church of God, which owned the Gospel Trumpet, would let out-of-town visitors who had business with the church, stay in one of the three spacious, upstairs rooms. Soon, the Gospel Trumpet found it needed more room and after moving to new quarters, one of the board of directors, David Caldwell, who is believed to have owned Caldwell Printing Co. (a news-paper organization), bought the house with his wife for one dollar from the church.

Years later, the Caldwell's sold the house to the in-laws of the current owners, John and Mary Lake*. The Lakes traded the home on Vineyard Street for their home in Illinois. The in-laws moved to Illinois and the Lakes moved to Anderson.

Along with the original house, the property contained a small out building that was once used as a restaurant. The Anderson Stove Works (built ca. 1900-1910) had facilities behind the house and the workers used to come to the building to eat hearty breakfast meals and sometimes lunches. The restaurant itself was two small rooms, presumably a small kitchen and a room as John said, was" not big enough to put two tables". Possibly, the workers took their lunch at a counter-type structure, or it is quite possible they simply ate outside. There is evidence of a sliding window such as a walk-up window might have. Eventually, the restaurant was disused and claimed by the earth again, and the stove works turned into Chesterfield Lumber, D & D Warehouse, Nik's, and now serves as a storage warehouse.

Although much of this history is physically gone, people who visited the home seem to be present.

The Lakes are deeply religious people with extremely good val-ues that they truly live by. Each of their children strive to keep the val-ues they've been taught, and more than one seem a little creeped out by the thought of the people who may be present but invisible in the home. When the Lakes bought the house, they moved into the former restaurant for a while and later moved into George Vineyard's house.

It was in this house, they raised 5 children (four boys and one girl), celebrated a long and happy marriage, and lived through decades of haunted activity. The experiences this family had were not a case of them coming on quickly and no trigger seems apparent, rather, these ghostly activities seem to be just a normal part of their lives.

Before the kitchen was remodeled, it housed an old telephone, "the black kind with bells". It never worked right by all accounts and when the kitchen was remodeled, understandably, the phone was taken out. During the remodel, a contractor, Skip, heard a telephone ring several times and would even tell the Lakes that the phone was ringing. Finally, once when Skip heard the ringing, John invited Skip to answer it. Skip was puzzled that no one was on the line, but attributed it to "just one of those things". After answering it two more times that day with the same results, Skip finally said, "I have to go," and he never returned.

Hearing bells isn't the only oddity in the kitchen. The appliances are modern, but during a kitchen remodel, an old refrigerator with a metal handle was hauled away. Since that time, they have heard the click of that old refrigerator handle in the kitchen and apparently at least one spirit seems unhappy with the switch in appliances. A visitor to the Lake's home dodged almost being struck by the vent cover flying off the new refrigerator as she entered to get a drink of water.

Another time, during a get-together at the Lake's home, a young guest named Jake* had an experience involving the kitchen,

"I was 10 years old and sitting in the living room at a get-together. Something said 'Jake'. I asked Mom if she called for me, but she said no. The pastors son, William came in and I asked him if he'd called my name. He said, 'No, but I heard it too. It was a shriek, kind of like a kid's voice.' Mom heard it too. It totally freaked William and me out."*

In both the kitchen and the one bathroom in the home, many times over the many years of raising five children, John would yell at the kids for leaving the water on. When they would check, generally the water would not be on. On one occasion, however, when they checked the kitchen, the water was running loudly.

The bathroom seems to be a haven for past guests of the home when it was used as lodging. Often, Josephine*, the only girl in a house full of boys, would be in the bathroom and watch the door open. She would think it was her brothers and yell at them, however, upon check-ing outside the door, Josephine found the hall empty. When they com-pared notes, the family realized all of them would experience the same things. "It didn't matter if you were using the toilet, at the sink or in the tub. The door would open as if someone were coming in, although you couldn't see anyone, and it would close as if someone were leaving." Additionally, many times Josephine's slumber party guests called out for her brothers as well, and even Josephine to stop playing tricks only to find that when they went to the door, no one was there.

Still, the bathroom and kitchen are not the only places for these spirits to roam. When Josephine's brothers got older and moved out, she took over their huge bedroom at the front of the house. This meant she had to go up the creaky stairs, around the left side turn left again into a small hall that lead to the large room, and consequently, was directly in front of the bathroom! Many times, she lay listening, because she heard footsteps in the hallway. "They weren't just creaks and squeaks. They were footsteps as if someone were walking. Sometimes, they would go into the bathroom, other times they went downstairs. Sometimes the steps came upstairs and ended at the doorway. I just hoped they didn't come in!" These same upstairs specters were heard by the whole fam-ily when everyone was downstairs. Kenny*, one of the Lake sons also said when he'd been in that same room, he'd hear footsteps stop just short of the door.

As the house was built during the Civil War, the basement is big, roomy, and creepy! For many years, one end of the basement held old canning jars. "When we finally got to cleaning up back there, we found old, really old jars of things. We couldn't tell what they had been or if they were from my grandmother or great-grandmother or something else!" Josephine remembers.

The coal room was also something that made the kids in the house apprehensive. It was a dark, empty foreboding room that was usually barred with a large wooden beam. Although John Lake denies there was any particular reason for the room to be closed, it did give the kids a reason to hurry with the chore of laundry in the basement.

Once when Mary was in the basement, John was sleeping up-stairs and Josephine was in bed, all three of them heard someone walk down the creaky stairs, open the front door, walk out and slam the door. Josephine heard her Mom call out for her, Josephine called out for her dad and her dad said he was in bed. They checked the front door and were very surprised to find the hook latch attached.

After all the boys moved out, the house still wasn't much quieter. Many times, the invisible guests could be heard walking from the dining room, into the living room and out the front door. It caused some confusion in the family, but the Lakes took it in stride. Once, when John was sitting on the couch in the living room, he heard the steps cross into the living room and go out the door, ending with a slam, but the door had not moved.

Eventually, Josephine married and moved out as well. John and Mary began caring for her father, whose wife had died four years earlier. They built a downstairs room for him off of the kitchen. One day in 1990, he came to her and said his wife, May, came to him at the foot of the bed and they talked for a while. He claimed May told him that it "wouldn't be too much longer" for him. Within the year, he died.

Although John indicated the activity decreased with the addition, and really stopped altogether after two boys next door started playing with a Ouija board and performing rituals with pentagrams, that may not be necessarily so. As John and Mary got older, they decided it was time to move down to that downstairs bedroom. John was lying on his side and Mary got up and out of bed. About the same time, a hand touched him and rolled him over on his back. When he looked to his side, nothing was there. Later in the room, Mary was playing solitary and John was on the bed. A cold breeze played over him, but she was warm. Many times, Mary felt cold breezes that went north to south in this room.

Despite these many occurrences, none of the family members seemed to be afraid, although they never tried to contact or talk to the guests either! While they are not disturbed by these guests, the family is not going to encourage or deny their existence. John, who is the strong leader of the family, hasn't been bothered by the "goings on", however, he likes to leave well enough alone.

George
Anderson, Indiana

The trouble next to the Lake's home (see *The Travelers*) started when a couple of young men, who rented the garage apartment, decided to play with a Ouija board and perform séances and rituals with the pentagram. They seemed to be performing rituals that leaned Satanic, however, Bill* and Janice*, the owners of the property, could not be sure. What they do know is that from that point on, "something different" was within the walls of the house.

It started when Janice's mother arrived for a visit, she was spooked by a door that kept opening and closing. Although no breeze was about and at times it was absolutely latched. Eventually, because of this activity, she didn't stay. One day she just packed her clothes, said she had enough and went home.

From that point on, the owners, who eventually named the disturbance 'George', were host to a paranormal show. Janice said she could "always tell when he came in- and when he left. He turned on lights, ran phantom fingers over arms and legs and made noises in virtually every part of the home."

Lila*, a very religious friend of the owners, was in the habit of visiting her friends quite often and had been going over for many weeks almost every day. Janice invited her to come in to a room because she wanted to show her something. The room, as Lila said, was "too dark for her", with its walnut furniture and crushed red velvet bedspread. Nonetheless, she stepped into the room and headed with Janice to the closet at the foot of the bed. They stood and talked about the room for a few minutes, and then Janice opened closet door. Lila, curious, went a few steps into the closet to see what Janice wanted her to look at. Janice pushed her farther into the closet.

"It may have come through the garage but that closet is the portal. It was cold and every hair on my body stood up. You could feel the evilness. I jerked away from Janice and said 'Don't you ever do something like that to me again.' It was unnerving. She had never told me anything about this thing that roamed their house before then. Janice started laughing and said, 'This is why I brought you up here. We have a ghost and

he comes in here a lot.' I looked at her and said, 'If I were you I'd put an open bible in every room in this house." Janice told me, 'I have, but he just goes through and closes them."

Although Lila was not sure if the "closing" of the bibles was gentle or if they were thrown and shut, she believes that whatever is in the house is not a ghost. As a very strong Christian woman, Lila believes these entities are demons and "that this one in particular is very active." For years she went over two to three times a week and stayed at the house till four or five in the morning. A lot of times nothing happened and the presence did not make itself known. She almost thought it was all a joke. Lila began sitting where things were to have happened just to make sure someone wasn't running in and doing the things. She felt it but she wanted to explain it.

"It roams continually. You might have a dark room and the lights will come on and yet, I sat where I can see all the light switches. One of his favorite things to do is to make the fan blades turn in the room off the dining room. He doesn't turn on the power but he "slaps" the blades hard to get them going. He likes to drag stuff and you can hear him bumping. I remember he would come down to the kitchen sink and mess around—you would hear noises and no one was there—it was continual. It had no qualms about being around people. I could hear him walking like he was 500 pounds!"

According to Lila, Janice swore the very first time she noticed George was during a house fire. It was then Janice saw him enter the house. From that point, George would touch many people in the house, rattle doors, open drawers and slam the bathroom door.

Sometimes Lila was afraid it would come home with her.

The last night she went to house was the holiday season she helped Janice wrap presents. Lila considers herself a saved person and says, "I know a demon can't bother me or enter me, but things can happen around me. The things I see are unsettling and I worry about the people involved in them. So many people look at it as a ghost, yet the Bible says people are in heaven when they die."

Until this point, Lila had just heard things, but never saw any physical manifestation. Despite her unease, she agreed to help wrap Janice's gifts. Lila and her teenage children, Maggie and Adam, went to Janice's house. Adam promptly fell asleep. Janice, Maggie and Lila continued wrapping gifts until about 3 a.m., joking and having a good time.

Janice keeps it hot- about 85 degrees -and then she would turn on gas stove and then open door… but when the thing was around, it would get cold. We heard a thumping like something like a trunk being dragged down each step. We sat for a second, looked at each other and looked at the stairway behind them at the same time. I had cold chills and my hair was standing up. As we looked back, my son who was sound asleep sat straight up, slowly looked that way too and that was the first time I saw a form come around stairway. It was a translucent vapor—white. The minute it came around the corner—it got that cold that fast," she said, snapping her finger. I told Janice, 'That's it. Maggie get our stuff.' I turned to Janice and said, 'I love you but I'm leaving. That's it. I finally saw it.' It was coming at us and had moved from the last rail coming toward the back door."

In the chaos, the figure had stopped moving forward and just hovered. For Lila it didn't matter that Janice would simply talk to it when it would come down, say "George, get your butt back upstairs!" and it would leave. She had enough. Before they could leave, they had to go by the door that they had seen him standing in front of. They had to wait for it to dematerialize and then they left.

In 2006, the owners of this haunted home moved out. Although it was said they moved because it was time to start a new phase in their lives after so many years in one place, one is left to ponder if George made himself *too* comfortable and finally overstepped even Janice's lenient boundaries.

Aqua Gardens
(aka Activity Center for Shadyside Park)
Anderson, Indiana

The tinny sound of music from the transistor radio drifted over the quiet night. It was well after dark and no one else but the group of teenagers was around.

Someone built a small fire and she could see several people roasting marshmallows. Nearly everyone was drinking beer. She shuddered, the cheap beer they could afford, or steal was not very good. Walking to the edge of the water, she looked into the shinning pool. It was so dark, so smooth, it almost looked like blood, she thought shuddering.

Suddenly, she was overrun by people and nearly lost her footing. Around her were naked bodies and clothes in crumpled piles. A small pink bra dangled precariously from part of the thin lace cup.
They were calling to her to get in and reluctantly she did so, pulling off her clothes where she stood. Trying to stay close to the shallow end, she relaxed and chatted with a couple of her friends. They decided to play water polo and she declined. The water was too deep.

She got caught up in watching the game, switching vantage points several times to get better views. Before she knew it, she was past her head in water. Despite trying to move back up to the surface, she couldn't stay afloat. Her head bobbed up and she saw her friends, still playing and unaware of her.

She went under water again and was silent.

Or so they say. Although there is no proof and in my research I have been unable to find any truth in the story, many versions of it exist. One involves Amy Chapman, who couldn't swim, but got in the water with everyone else. It was dark and no one could see very well. Amy must have stepped in a hole or into deeper water and drowned while everyone else was splashing and yelling. No one heard her cries for help. Her body was found floating at daybreak. Another involves children, a young man and yet another version has a man and woman committing suicide Romeo and Juliet style.

Regardless of the legends, what we do know is that Aqua Gardens was purchased from Meyer Sand & Gravel (IMI) by Anderson in 1970 and renamed Shadyside Recreation Center. I do remember in the early 1970s that Aqua Gardens seemed to be closed, but perhaps that was for the trails to be put in. Later I remember hearing kids playing in the area and wishing I were allowed to be there as well. The people in town always said it was haunted and children were cautioned about going back to Aqua Gardens.

As if the legend wasn't a cautionary tale in itself, paranormal activities have occurred. The rest of the legend states that she is seen covered in algae looking over the water. Some people say they've seen her warn people away. One story I heard as a child was that she would float on the water at night to keep people out.

For Matthew, the legend may hold somewhat true. He fully admits he was out after dark. "It was a nice night and I wanted to take a walk." He's never been one to be afraid of what lurks on trails or in the dark. "I can take care of myself."

Matthew is a young man in his mid-20s. He used the trails with his chocolate lab, Nayla, on a regular basis. "I held on to my Nayla leash and started to jog at a brisk pace. She kept up – which was expected – but as we rounded the section near the old Aqua Marine area, Nayla whimpered. I didn't know if some rabbit or other critter was in the brush but I kept going. Nayla didn't. I damn near fell on my ass."

He laughed and continued, "It was real funny. She is never afraid of anything. She's a 60 pound dog! But she was that night. She got down on the ground and kind of bowed. She's never done that since."

What happened next made Matthew rethink walking with his dog after dark. "She walked out of the water. Naked. I'm one to enjoy a pretty figure but I could tell something wasn't right. She was wet with water and pale- her skin almost glowed from the water and how pale she was. But her look was blank. She was coming towards us. Nayla was giving out a high pitched yelp. I could only stand and stare."

"She crossed the path in front of us. I nervously said, 'Hello'. The girl turned her head towards me. I could see through her but I could see her eyes had the white part but where the colored part should be, she had a solid black shape, like her pupil had taken over the entire colored section. Her lips, despite the water, looked dry and almost swollen. The girl's mouth opened, but no sound came out. Only water. And she disappeared. I looked down at my shoe and it was wet. Nayla had gotten off her belly but she was standing next to me, shivering."

Matthew and Nayla went back to the car, "quickly". And didn't venture out to the pond for a long time.

Sixth Street's Priest House
1220 W.6th Street, Anderson, Indiana

The house sat empty and abused for years. Not much is currently known about the home except it was originally built by the Priest family, which seems to be some of the earliest settlers in the Anderson area. In the history books, the Priest family was apparently not bound for local fame, nor were they considered "prominent", however, they were by all accounts a relatively well off, clannish group of people, who believed in taking care of their family. One can see through various records that the family was large, having seven children. As the years went on, these children grew up and moved away. Later in life, documents show that the children came back to live in the home and to also take care of their parents. Apparently they were progressive as well, in allowing their daughters freedom to make marital choices- or not.

After the Priest parents died, the children sold the land and the house. The land was subdivided in to the newest addition to the city of Anderson and the home changed hands many times over the years. In the mid 1970s, the home was subdivided and became yet another statistic in the slum lord syndrome that so plagues many older homes. By the 1980s, the home was decrepit, but anyone who looked at it could see the charm and appeal it could have.

Situated just two blocks north of Historical 8th Street in Anderson, this 4000 square foot home boasted a large wooden floored front porch in the 1980s. At that time, the home appeared to be a Queen Anne, however, some details seemed to indicate it was much older. Large, wavy glassed windows over 5 feet tall and nearly as wide graced the front facade. The upstairs windows were 5 feet long and in the middle of the house on the upper floor was a beautiful oval window. Black, hand hewn shutters hung on all the windows.

Inside, the house had been chopped up many times, but one could see the former grandeur. Solid wooden floors shined hazily in the now dingy rooms. One could see the 1920s kitchen from the front room of the house.

The floor of the kitchen was black and white checkerboard, scraped and scratched with heavy use and the tall narrow cabinets that held dishes, still held their dignity. The grand, wide oak and cherry staircase had been viciously cut in half, one part sent to the local dump. The upstairs was moderately better, in that in the doorless bathroom, was a 6 feet long cast iron bathtub. Each room upstairs had a door on every available inside wall. The oval window from the outside was blocked in the hallway that divided the upstairs by a newly constructed wall. The oval window was now in a closet.

The house was not a happy place for most tenants. No air conditioning in summer. Poorly heated in the winter from a sole radiant heater in each apartment which left the room with the heater stifling and which left the rest of the apartment cold. The windows were dirty and the frames eaten by bugs. But still, the house had a feeling. Most of the people who rented the home had little money, had few options and were taken advantage of by the landlord.

The attic itself was a master work, with balloon framing, which suggests pre-Civil War construction; one could have put in another apartment with its twelve foot tall ceilings. However, it was left barren and no one ventured there for long.

The first documented case of a haunting was when I lived there shortly after I was married. I was becoming very sensitive, fell in love with the house, and suspected it was haunted, but at the time I didn't want to acknowledge that side of my personality.

"I was not comfortable in certain parts of the upper apartment during certain times of the day and night. I was not comfortable in the downstairs apartment under what would have been our stairway. In the late afternoon, unfortunately when it was dinner time, I could not bring myself to be in the kitchen for long or I had to make sure my husband was around, just for company. Something bad happened in the kitchen. The feel radiated to the room across the hall and into our bedroom as well.

When my ex-husband and I had been married for about 6 months and had already had several quarrels, he left the apartment. As I sat in the living room and cried, I thought about how insanely stupid the fight was and became annoyed with myself and the horrid selection of television programs on my cable-less television. The shadows grew longer and early evening turned into darkness. I watched the television flicker and wondered when and if my husband would come back. In that moment, I sensed something in the hallway.

Looking out of the corner of my eye, I thought it was just the light of the television flickering over the outdated wood paneling or the curtain that separated the hallway from my bedroom. As I looked out of the corner of my eye, I realized the figure did not conform to the shape of the curtain and it didn't flicker in time with the television. Slowly, I turned and faced the shape head on. It was a woman, dressed in a prairie skirt, and long sleeved blouse. I sensed rather than saw color. Her clothing was light brown and cream colored, well laundered and very worn. I watched her face and saw her expression change from one of going about her business to extreme confusion and then to annoyance. She seemed to be puzzled and mad at the wall that had been built, which blocked her from walking the entire length of the hallway and looking out of the oval window. Even as I was watching her, hoping she didn't turn her annoyance to me, I thought, 'Oh my god, I can see all her features!' She looked milk white but all of her bones of her angular face and ridges and pleats of her skirt were outlined in gray shadow as though an artist had sketched her and used shadowing.

Fascinated, I watched the annoyed woman turned to the left, go through the curtain and disappeared into my bedroom."

Elusive for sure, despite looking into the history of the house, it's been impossible to track this woman down. No pictures exist from former owners, it seems and the house has had dozens of tenants since it stopped serving as a single family home. One interesting tidbit of information that gives some insight into who the Priests may have been was the discovery of a simple straw hat that was discovered trapped between the floor joists during a 1988-1989 remodel of the upstairs unit. The hat was made of yellow woven straw, with a black crushed velvet ribbon tied in a wide pressed bow around it. In the top, was an intentional hole. Upon more investigation, it was found to be a 'suffragist hat', worn by women in the 1900 to 1920 period. The hole was to accommodate their hair buns.

A study of the premises did not turn up any video or photo anomalies, however an EVP of a woman was present. She seems to say, "Well, get on with it then," and later, "I don't see anything." Perhaps she was arguing with someone or maybe she was curious in what was going on in the house. I went by the property earlier this year. It looks so forlorn. I am sad for this house. Someone obviously loved it and built it to last. The windows are now small and ugly. The soffits and sills are starting to rot. I looked in the back door and saw that someone was remodeling, but looked like the remodeling had long since been abandoned, like the house. Hopefully, this property can be more fully investigated and the mysterious nature of its visitors and voices more clearly understood.

The Priest house of 6th Street in Anderson, Indiana.

Kelly's House

Pierce Street, Alexandria, Indiana

Not a lot of history is known about that house on Pierce Street. Unassuming, comfortable and full of love, no one would ever suspect from looking at the outside that the inside held such scary treats.

Three generations of family have experienced ghostly activity in the house. The owner, Kelly, has seen a girl in a flowing white gown in the house on many occasions including the kitchen and hallway. The first time Kelly saw the girl, Kelly had been the homeowner for a short time. She was in the restroom. Kelly saw the ethereal glow out of the corner of her eye, saw the girl who was about 10 years old and in a flowing white gown. Then she was gone. Then Kelly turned back because she thought someone was in the house and the girl was there again.

Kelly told herself that she shouldn't turn completely away but just look out of the corner of her eye and the girl remained standing there. In subsequent sightings, the girl did not. She touches Kelly's hands in the kitchen near the sink. Kelly also saw her under the kitchen table. Once, the girl tugged Kelly's long blond hair. Kelly described it as "playful." Throughout this period, she would find things in the house moved, and no one in the family would cop to it. When I went to her house for her daughter's birthday, I was going into Kelly's bedroom to pick up my coat and my arm was jerked behind me by unseen hands. It made my day!

Kelly, a religious woman, isn't completely sure what to believe. She doesn't like to necessarily play with the ghosts or bring them out. What has worked for her is saying that it is ok for the girl to be in the house as long as she doesn't scare Kelly's family. "We won't bother you, you don't bother us."

Her son, Zach used to use the restroom with the door closed because of the girl. Once, he had a dream when he was very young. In the dream, he heard a noise and opened the door to his room. He looked into the living room and saw a girl in a rocking chair. She told him he should pull up the floor boards in the house because there was a diamond under them. Although tempted, the family never did as suggested.

Years later, when he was older, Zach came home with his friend

Jeremiah. As they approached the house, they saw a shadow run from the living room to the hallway. Knowing the rest of the family to be out for the evening, the pair stayed outside for a while and finally got the courage up to inside- and saw no evidence of anyone or the shadow!

Another time, Zach was working on a computer in the living room and he felt the ground shake like someone was walking in the house. He looked around, but no one else was in the house. Even the dogs were sleeping. He put his headphones back on and felt it again. He ignored it, trying to blow it off as a result of something outside the house.

Suddenly, he felt someone brush his shoulder. He took his headphones off again and heard his name called several times. Slowly, a hooded figure materialized in the hallway, looking directly at him. It was about 5'10" inches tall. Zach said, "I didn't feel like I was in imme-diate danger, but I left for the night."

Zach was into astral projection and recounted his first astral projection experience. He messaged me about 9:40 p.m. on March 24, 2012. He said he'd projected for the first time and saw himself lying in bed. He went into the kitchen where he saw a girl about 15 or 16 years old curled in a ball under the table. She was wearing a 1950s dress that was had wide gauzy straps word on the upper arm. He asked the girl why she was crying and she told Zach that she couldn't find her family. Zach noticed the girl was crying. Crying tears of blood. "Her eyes were black and bleeding."

I asked him the usual questions regarding drugs and alcohol. He assured me he had imbided in neither. "I even stayed away from caffeine all day so I could concentrate better, " he said.

As we analyzed the event, he said she was the same girl seen in overalls that told him to rip up the floor in his room. Once he saw her eyes, he "freaked out and woke up." Zach was afraid to say anything to his mom because he didn't want her to freak out at his methods to reach "enlightenment" through meditation and astral projection.

We agreed it seemed that this girl came to him because she could identify with him, possibly because of his age. At one time, Kelly thought the girl was in the house because of the baby she'd lost a long time ago. She thought it might be the baby growing up in a parallel world. That evening, Zach said he was either going to have his friend, Kevin, spend the night or he was going over to Kevin's house.

For me, what is even better is that even though Zach is still living in the house, his nephew has also had experiences. Carson started talking about a "girl" in his playpen at a very young age. To be that articulate as a toddler is amazing. Then he started having issues when he took his nap. Over a period of a couple weeks, he had several events like this one.

His mother, Liz, heard him say, "Quit! Stop!"

Liz asked, "What's going on?"

Carson replied, "She's hitting me."

"Who's hitting you?"

"The litter girl." Apparently, the girl hit Carson because she didn't want to play.

Liz took him out of the playpen and asked if he wanted Mamaw to get rid of her.

Kelly went in and used a stern voice telling the girl she had to go. Since then, they have not had any events in the house.

Interestingly, Kelly's ex-husband and her current one, Howard, haven't experienced anything in the house.

In retrospect, we're still uncertain of how many spirits are in the house. Did the girl grow as Zach and Liz did? Was the little girl the daughter of the 1950s spirit or was she the mother of the little girl? And what about the shadow and hooded figure Zach encountered? Were these just spirits passing through as if in a portal? Were they spirits brought in by others in the house?

Despite these hauntings, the home continues to be a place of laughter and love for many generations.

Laying Hays Cemetery to Rest
Wilkinson, Indiana

We've seen them in movies and books- a full moon, a graveyard and chaos usually results. Hancock County has received the notoriety and unwanted attention that Hays Cemetery has found. Many stories about this cemetery exist and this book can't begin to capture them all.

At many of our ghost tours, we've had people ask about Hays Cemetery. For people who have grown up in Madison County, it is known as the infamous Main Street Graveyard. It was nicknamed Main Street Graveyard because to get to it, you take Main Street from Anderson and drive into Hancock County.

Although this qualifies as a very backroads story, it is also a very unfortunate product of irresponsibility. As far back as the 1960s, it's been a hangout for teenagers throughout the decades. A place to hang-out turned to a place to party and from there a monstrous amount of desecration including burning, spray painting and defecation occurred. So much has happened that there are numerous missing stones or only fragments shattered beyond repair are left behind.

According to Sue Baker, author of Hancock County's definitive guide to cemeteries, the entrance to the cemetery is "on a narrow lane and easily missed during the growing season". At one time, the road that leads into the cemetery was host to a tile works and a steam saw mill. This cemetery is host to over 250 burials, although less than a third of those stones remain, largely due to vandalism.

In the 1970s, groups of teenagers with nothing to do and looking for a scare used to go out to Hancock County's version of Cry Baby Bridge, which is very near Hays Cemetery. Every state seems to have one of these bridges; some states seem to have several. This particular version of Cry Baby Bridge is metal and starts with a woman who has a car crash and her baby dies. When you stop on the bridge you are supposed to hear the baby. Other versions of this go much the same except more babies die, the woman died and you hear her too, the woman comes up out of the water with her baby in her arms, and the baby and mother push your car off the bridge if you stop and shut off the motor. Sometimes, if you put powder on the back of your car, you are supposed to see the hand prints of the babies, the mother or even both after they've pushed you off the bridge and onto the road.

To enhance this experience, many times, on the way to Cry Baby Bridge, teens would stop off at Mt. Giliad church and run around the church 10 times before going to both the bridge and the cemetery. It was supposed to help "conjure spirits".

Finally, to round this experience off, teens would go into Hays Cemetery and party- often drinking, playing music, and using drugs. When they became bored with those activities, they turned to running over stones, throwing them, breaking them into pieces or even stealing them.

Lozen*, an Indiana-born, former Hays Cemetery visitor, recounted the following story:

"No one wanted to drive down the lane because your car got stuck in mud. The trees on the left were said to contain the souls of still birth babies who had been buried in the cemetery. If you parked you could hear "group babies crying.

When you entered the cemetery, you wanted to turn your car around and back in so that you couldn't be seen from the road. We used to walk back because the road was so muddy. Somewhere in the late 60s or 70s, an old lady moved back there with her son. I am not sure if she was related to the original farm or to someone who owned land close by. An old man who lived near would chase people out. He was the one people said shot arrows at you or would shoot at you with a gun.

I tried to find out who the lady was, but I couldn't find the name of her or her son or how she got into the abandoned building to the back right corner of the cemetery. It might have been a converted outbuilding that was converted into basic living space. The building was secluded for sure. I guess her son was considered "slow".

Supposedly, her son went off killing people who were partying and visiting late at night. The story went that he stuck their heads on stones. Before he snapped, he used to go hunting to help mom out and used either an axe or arrows. His ghost is supposed to roam the cemetery. I know in 1981 there was a remnant of a barn or some other structure to the right of the cemetery.

Another story in the 1970s involves some people that went back into the cemetery and found out people lived there—the son and his mom. Later they went back and terrorized them I don't know how many times, but supposedly the mother was raped and murdered- the son may have been outside at the time. But he came back and killed the guys back there. I am not sure what happened to the son. His ghost can shoot arrows or use a double-headed ax. He would kill anyone who was going to hurt his mom or the graveyard. If it's true, maybe she was hiding from a bad husband. There was supposed to have a garden with shack, but I never saw it. They were also supposed to have some chickens.

When we went to the cemetery, someone had trashed and bashed tombstones. Broken knives were all over—in trees, some rusty and a devil face was carved on one tree, which I just thought was not good.

I found ponytail holders with metal balls on them that for some reason freaked me out, like something bad had happened to the owner of them. I got a bad vibe off one of them. It was looped around a knife stuck in a tree. I took the ponytail holder and as I touched it, I saw girl with brown hair.

I grabbed the knife out of tree and saw it was a hunting knife. It was wide, thick and had a thin blade—9 inches—I really had to wiggle it to it get out. The others weren't hunting knives.

They were butcher knives, maybe 6 inches long, not serrated and maybe 2 inches wide. A lot of rusty ones were on the ground. All had wooden handles with brass screws. The broken ones were on the edge of the woods, trees, etc. Once, I found a ring- an elongated diamond shaped sapphire. It had a circle of diamonds like Lady Diana's engagement ring.

The cemetery just made me sad and it gave off a 'funk'. I took all the knives out of the trees and put them on the ground.

Supposedly, there was a stone with a skull on it, but that was a crock. At the time, people were still putting flowers out on the graves and the flowers and urns were tipped and broken."

Later, in the 1980s, the tradition continued. Long before the stricter cemetery rules we are fortunate to have today, it became the place to be on a Friday night. Dares were made and many car-loads of high schoolers were found leaving the big Anderson cruising spots of Broadway and the Mounds Mall, opting to see if they could provoke the old man or if they could actually see the boy going from stone to stone.

The largest two offenders were Anderson High School and Madison Heights High School students. Every Halloween, a story about the graveyard seemed to run in the paper. In the 1983 Anderson High School X-Ray newspaper, Steve Bannon and Elizabeth Ann Reeder dared readers to "travel across Baby Doll Bridge then venture into Main Street Graveyard on a full-moon midnight." They added to the already countless stories by claiming that crossing Baby Doll Bridge (now Cry Baby Bridge) would yield the sounds of babies crying.

If you went into the graveyard on a foggy night, stayed for "at least an hour" and let your windows frost up, footprints of babies would appear. Additionally, if you put a baby doll on your dashboard and leave the car, when you returned the doll was said to have tears of blood on its face. Still they also said that if you went into the graveyard, you shouldn't be surprised if you were greeted by a Black Maria. It was supposed to circle around the cemetery waiting to convey anyone who was left behind. Finally, some teenagers reported going to the cemetery and having a hatchet embedded in the top of their car by some unknown force.

In a 1988 on a nocturnal trip out to Hays Cemetery, one pair of ladies were completely surprised by the slightly sinister atmosphere of their encounter. Wendy and Renee were very good friends. Wendy was a bookworm and very science driven. She was a "semi-prep" and Renee was punk. Where Renee was adventurous Wendy generally shied away and played it safe.

After negotiating the heavily vegetated path up to the cemetery, Renee and Wendy finally arrived. Renee was kind enough to disclose their experience in an interview:

"We arrived at the very dark cemetery around midnight. The road was so rutted, it was hard for the little Mazda to make its way deeper into the cemetery. When we rounded the curve that lead up the hill, the headlights fell on two people standing in front of a very large stone. They were dressed in black, had dark hair and had pale skin. Wendy stopped her car and I jumped out. I had waited so long to see what the fuss was about. I started looking at stones, not seeing much because of how dark it was. What I could see was in the headlights of Wendy's car.

I remember I was to the east side of the people standing by the stone. As I was walking through the section inside the drive-

way loop, I head Wendy calling to me.

As I thought, she wanted to go. I was so bummed. It seemed to take forever to get there and then I'd been there for all of about ten minutes- that wasn't time for anything to happen!

Wendy called again and said, "We need to go- NOW."

I told her to wait just a second—I wanted at least a few more minutes in the cemetery. I heard the purr of her car coming around. I turned to look at her and she gritted out,

'We are going. I am going. Now.' She nudged her head in the direction of the two people we'd seen as we arrived.

Walking towards the car, I looked at them. Where they were standing was very dark, but I could see they turned and were looking at us. Their eyes glowed red! Trying to walk calmly, I got into the car and Wendy took off before I'd even had a chance to close the door.

As we went back down the lane, I asked her, 'did you see what I saw?'

She replied, 'There has to be an explanation.'

That night, we tried to sort it out but came up with nothing. After that night, Wendy wouldn't talk about it again still won't to this day."

From the 1990s, the cemetery fell into greater disrepair. A new generation of kids made Hays Cemetery the place to party. Rumors flew on the Internet that the cemetery contains the grave of a little girl suspected to be the devil or at least be a pawn of his. Supposedly at her grave, there was a plant that grew like a pitchfork.

In 2000, the American Ghost Society (AGS) reported on a website that they performed an "investigation" on this cemetery. The author, Kathy Harlow, reported she was "curious as to why a cemetery would be located at least a quarter mile off the road, having to drive down a long forsaken dirt path, in the middle of a secluded wooded area, next to a very steep ravine, situated in the middle of nowhere." She went on to say, "to describe this location is to describe the makings of a haunted movie. Entering at night is definitely for the bold hearted."

Haunted movie, indeed. Never mind that houses exist as close as a quarter of a mile away. Never mind that Harlow and her group may have been trespassing in a protected area well after the time most cemeteries are closed to the public. During the course of their visit,

Harlow claimed "If I walked, I heard footsteps. If I stopped, the footsteps stopped." The investigators I interviewed did not find anything out of the ordinary with this phenomenon. Aside from feelings of "uneasiness", nothing more was found at the site by Harlow.

As the members of group went on to Crybaby Bridge, Harlow had a camera malfunction and heard a "kerplunk" in the water, although the source was never seen. Later, as they were driving away from the graveyard, her EMF detector went off. Harlow was convinced she was giving a ride to a ghost.

Also reported in the Harlow article was a story that a man murdered his wife by hanging and then shot her with an arrow, that graves have fallen down the ravine and that Satanists used bodies for their sacrifices in the 70s.

According to an entry at Morbidrequiem's Live Journal, the person went to the cemetery at night in August 2006 and found "a large number of the trees that looked as though they had been caught on fire…at one place in the graveyard we found a patch of ground where no grass was growing. This patch was in the shape of a cross."

Unfortunately, Harlow and Morbidrequium were unaware of the history of that dirt path and the one that curved off of it and into the woods close to the ravine. According to a member of the Hays family, the land was part of two 40-acre land grants from Andrew Jackson. As Mary Mays wrote:

> "The Hermitage in Tennessee is built on land that was once owned by the Hays family. Jackson and the Hayses were friends and neighbors in the Carolina territory and he took in young John C. Hays when his father Hugh Hays Jr. died of the wounds he received during a battle in the Indian Wars in 1812. He was probably serving alongside Jackson at the time.
>
> John C. married Hannah Blakely in 1831 in Washington County, Tennessee, and they moved to Hancock County, Indiana in 1832. The land was granted to them in two separate parcels, one 40-acre parcel in 1834 and the other 40-acre parcel in 1835. The cemetery at that time was on land owned by the McQueary's in 1831, and the earliest grave that is dated is that of Rachel McQueary, wife of James, who died in 1834. There were some other stones marking graves that were just that - stones with initials on them - but no dates or full names.

The McQueary land was next to the Hays land, so in essence, the Hays Cemetery is adjacent to the Hays Homestead.

The woods next to the Cemetery is all that is left of the farm, and my brother inherited that when my dad died. John C. Hays was buried there in 1863, his wife Hannah in 1868, and four of their young children, James in 1837, Samuel in 1838, Hugh in 1842, and Rachel in 1854. They had four other children who grew to adults. One of them, my great-grandfather, Robert Rankin Hays bought a section of the cemetery in 1885, and in the deed it refers to the cemetery as the Garriott Cemetery. My great great-grandparents (John C. and Hannah), my great-grandparents (Robert R. and Mary Eliza), my grandfather Clarence McPherson Hays, and my parents Daniel Ward and Annie Laurie Hays are buried there."

Mary thought maybe her father could have been the man who chased kids, but she was adamant that he would have never used a weapon— "that was just not his way!"—however, she did write laughingly that if her brother had been there during the time the kids were there, "he would have been more likely to party *with* them" at the time. Additionally, she was sure if her father would have had any experiences on the property, he would have told the family.

Mary had no experiences with the Hays Cemetery or property, although she demurely hinted, but did not elaborate on a Hays Family legend about a family member who was a spiritualist and haunted the old Hays home. She did however, recount a story from 1964. "I remember walking down to the bridge with my brother. It was foggy and cold and we allowed the spookiness of the bridge to scare us. We ran all the way back to the farmhouse laughing and out of breath."

So where does this information leave us?

Since 2001, Hays cemetery has been listed on the Indiana Pioneer Cemetery Restoration Project (INPCRP) Hall of Shame, however, the pictures listed on the website do not reflect the five years of preservation efforts which have occurred. It hasn't been an easy road. In the five years that have passed, the cemetery has seen a turn around. At one time the lane was shaded and overgrown with trees and vegetation. In recent years, the trees have been cut back in order to curb vandalism and the stones are visible from the road in the winter time. Also, the stones for the most part have been reset and cleaned of graffiti and the broken fragments have been placed in a garden of lost history to one side of the graveyard. No longer are there knives in trees, trash, or ruts in the road.

Still the legends persist. Could there be any truth to the stories that abound about Hays Cemetery?

We began by going to Mt. Giliad and running as suggested in some of the stories we were given. While it was good exercise, it proved to be nothing more.

When we conducted a daytime investigation of this cemetery, there was no evidence of any more supposed sacrifices taking place, nor were there any men with hatchets, bows, guns or any other weapon to chase us. No evidence of a pitchfork plant or stone was evident, although there are several small children buried there. We conducted several experiments with footsteps on different parts of the cemetery. On the gravel, we seemed to pick up an echo of our footsteps- which promptly stopped when we ceased walking. Our EMF detectors picked up nothing abnormal.

We went to the cemetery a week after Morbidrequiem's nocturnal visit, and we found no evidence of any dirt or any other type of cross. We would have suspected, even if the grass had been growing between the two visits, that some evidence of the cross would remain due to the grass not having much time to grow. There were equally unstartling results at Crybaby Bridge- although we did see a few frogs jump into the water.

We also researched newspapers, talked with other people in the community and searched police reports. To our knowledge and exhaustive research, we have found no evidence to support any deaths or killing in the cemetery or the land surrounding it that would match those in the legends told to us.

In our opinion, no investigation is ever closed, but aside of a spirit of family and home, most of the stories can be explained away or attributed to nerves or teenage hype.

As this cemetery experiences more interest from historians and preservation groups, it is also continually protected by land owners, the township trustee, police and neighbors. Anyone trespassing after dusk will be asked to leave and/or arrested.

A burnt tree stump serving as a grim reminder of the destruction that has occurred at this cemetery.

The stone garden at Hays Cemetery. Bits of broken stones were put here to try and preserve some of the living history the stones represent. When we were there, we counted over 20 stones.

Baby Doll Bridge, otherwise known as Cry Baby Bridge.

Where it all started
Anderson, Indiana

I was about nine years old when I first became aware of ghosts. I never gave them much thought past Casper when I was really young. When I first became aware of ghosts, we had just moved into our parents' dream home in the country. The three acres that came with it were nothing to brag about. About one acre total was covered in cement. At one time the property had boasted 153 acres. It had been the Fiburns/Skyles farm for many years. About a quarter mile south of our house, a log cabin stood as the first house on the property. At one time a working dairy farm had been housed there as well as a pig farm. The remnants of the cattle feed trough were there as well. The cut off posts would have held a roof and the silo bases would have had a silo capable of delivering a fermented blend of grain that smelled sweetly of olives for the cattle. It was a self-sufficient farm, producing food from a garden and it even had a spring house for cool items. As there was no creek or running water nearby, chunks of ice would have been placed in the spring house to keep dairy products. In the 1940s, the family began to sell small parcels of the property.

By the time our family arrived on the scene, dissension amongst the Skyles clan and the Filburns existed. They weren't mad at us per se, however, they were unhappy that the house had been sold to "non-family" folks. Indeed it was an eclectic group of people who had owned the property. The oldest Mrs. Skyles used to keep the freezer and pantry full and she would lock up the food and dole it out when necessary. Additionally, she related a story to my sister about a Ouija board incident. Apparently she had been playing with a Ouija board with her sisters and her mom found out. Her mother was not happy, especially when she found out that the planchette had moved and some other undisclosed odd things happened. Mrs. Skyles mother made her and her sisters sweep the entire house "to get rid of the spirits".

For us, the house meant, spirits or not, room for chickens, dogs, cats, and later ponies. Part of a larger overall farm, the house boasted the covered remnants of a one room schoolhouse in the "parlor" or the "room with the fireplace" as we always called it. My sisters, Mary and Lorri, didn't like the room. For them, it was fortunate family didn't spend much time in this room, despite its large brick covered fireplace. We spent more time in the family room in front of the television. The rest of the house had undergone some aesthetically displeasing makeover somewhere in the 50s and now in the 70s. However, this house was huge, which completely made up for any shortcomings in beauty. Plus there was a large tire swing, a big barn to explore and several mulberry trees from which to munch berries. So we forgave the house.

Our parents were not the most sociable of people. My mother was a stay at home mom, very religious, had few outside friends and seemingly few outside interests. My father was not religious, worked two jobs most of my life and also had few outside interests. They seemed to have large ups and downs in their relationship, which culminated in a divorce in 1989.

While our father was largely invisible in our lives because he worked so much, our mother was very visible. Her word was law and you didn't dare step outside of it. Consequently, from my standpoint, my relationship with her was not very nurturing and so that, coupled with her view of the paranormal and the Catholic church, I never really discussed ghosts with her. The one time I did talk about it, she said, "There are no such things!" and that, was conveniently that!

When we moved in, several items went missing. My miniature working 7-up dispenser. My sister's precious talcum powder. Many of our beloved stuffed animals. When the items weren't found after we moved in, my sister's and I chalked it up to Mom weeding out our things before we moved.

As part of the purchase agreement, the German Baptist folks we bought the home from were responsible for correcting the wavy hardwood floors. I could have cried when I realized that they built another floor of two by fours and plywood over the existing floors. When we had originally looked at the house, I really loved the floors and the sound my shoes made as I walked across it. Nevertheless, in went the bad 70s renovation, which also left us with green shag carpet and fake wood paneling over the plaster walls.

Although we were already moved into the home, renovations were still taking place which meant we girls had to sleep on the couches and rollaway beds in our family room. After waking up one morning and wanting to find some toys, my sister's and I came across a couple books. They were like the Golden Books that most children at the time had, but these were different. They weren't square, nor were they as thin and new as ours. The shape followed the top of the tree on the cover and the pages were much thicker than normal books. They were really good books with beautiful illustrations. Our mother came in and saw us reading together-playing together was quite unusual- and she told us we could finish looking at the books, but they had to go back to the owners.

We were all pretty bummed about it, but, when the daughter of the former owner came to visit her grandfather next door, we tried to give her the books. We told her thank you but that the books needed to stay with her. She looked puzzled and said the books weren't hers. We were kind of dumbfounded and knew if we didn't give the books back, our mom might get mad so we gave them to her anyway and she somewhat reluctantly took them.

Later that evening as we got ready for bed, we went to find yet another something from our boxes in the fireplace room. I saw the books we'd returned tucked on a box. I asked my sisters if they took them back and they said no. We moved them to the bottom of one of the boxes and hoped they'd stay there until mom forgot about them. We never saw them again.

A couple of months after we moved in, when we were all settled in our rooms and unpacked, my mother called a local Catholic priest to come and bless our home. Father Fennessy was a fairly young priest from St. Mary's Catholic Church, in Anderson. I think as a child I had a short-lived crush on him because he looked slightly like Paul McCartney. He came in and went from room to room chanting prayers and dousing the place in holy water. What we didn't know at the time was that he had his own demons to combat.

As you went up our stairs, there was an old plank wooden door at the end of a short hall that led to the attic. On either side of the attic door were our rooms. Lorri had her own room on the right side, because she was the oldest. My sister Mary and I slept in the same room on the left side. One day, a couple of years after we moved in, Lorri came downstairs late, which was kind of odd. She was the one up at dawn to feed the ponies and get the day started. She asked Mary and me if we'd been in her room. Of course we said no. She asked again, and again we said no. She was a little perturbed because she said she was positive that "someone came in Mom's purple coat". We suggested it might have been mom or dad, and she said no, it was too tall.

Mary was a little creeped out, thinking, "why would mom go upstairs and do that? Why wouldn't she take the coat off first?" I was pretty much not buying it. I figured my two older sisters were just up to have a little fun with their little sister. Soon, we all went on with our day and forgot about the conversation. More time passed and when I was about 11 or 12 years old, I had my second conversation about the unexplained. I had been watching Sammy Terry (a play on "ceme-tery"), who was a local television host for scary and sometimes really sub-B movies on Friday and Saturday night. After staying up way into the night watching movies, I was too scared to put my feet on the floor and go through the dark fireplace room, up the steep stairs, and past the creepy attic door to my own room. I was too scared to go to the restroom, which was about 25 feet away!

With a full bladder I slept till about 8:00 a.m. As I was contem-plating the move to the restroom, my sister Mary asked me, "All bullshit aside, did you sleep down here all night?" I answered affirmatively. She went into the kitchen to make breakfast and when she came into the family room again, she asked me, "Did you really sleep down here last night?"

I repeated my statement.

Mary broke down and told me the following story:

"I went to bed scared. I'd felt scared all evening and really couldn't sleep. When I finally did get in bed, I moved the covers up to my shoulders so just my head was sticking out. I looked at the window and I moved my eyes to the picture of Jesus. The gold frame was glowing. Then I saw it. There was this dark cloaked monk-like figure at the foot of the bed with no face. He had a brown cloak with a hood on and I couldn't see his face or hands. His brown robe had a knot where it was belted around his waist and two knots on the ends of each string. I was so scared and couldn't move. I tried to move, but I just couldn't. I watched as it went to your bed and sat down. It said, "Nikki is downstairs asleep. Not to worry- I am here with you." I was really scared after that, and still couldn't move, so I moved my eyes around. Eventually, I could move and I rolled onto my side, so I was facing it, just to keep an eye on it and I must have fallen asleep. When I woke up, it was light outside and there was a butt print on the bed."

I said, "No way—I gotta check this out!" And sure enough, there was a butt print on the bed. Again, I was skeptical. I really thought my sisters were bamming me and trying to get me to be scared. I asked Mary to sit down because I thought for sure she'd done it, but the print didn't match. I could tell that Lorri wouldn't be a match either. I didn't believe fully, but the seed had been planted.

From that point on, I read every book on paranormal topics that I could get my hands on. During this time, it was pretty much a historical account of people like King Henry the Eighth and Vlad the Impaler. However, there was an excellent book about the Borley Rectory. It was from these books that I opened my mind to things that were not cut and dried. I loved the idea that something could be around without us knowing it.

The event that really solidified my belief in the paranormal was a sleepover when I was 13. Mary and I were getting along better and we had the same friend set, so we decided to have a big slumber party. Having not much to do out in the country and with a mother who was largely unwilling to drive us into town, we had to make due with what we could on our property. We went for long walks, talked, yelled at cars- all the normal things teenage girls do. We decided to sleep downstairs in the fireplace room because we couldn't decide how to arrange all of us in our room.

That night, my life changed forever.

I must have been tired after all the excitement. I was the first asleep and one by one we all fell asleep. Mary was the last asleep. Later, Mary woke up and heard Elena. She was talking to someone in Spanish. It sounded like a conversation but sounded like she was "agitated" and nervous. The more Mary talked to her the more aggressive her tone got. "It was like I was interrupting." Mary told me, "Finally, I said, 'Elena what are you doing? Who are you talking to? Elena? Elena?' When she was done talking, I said 'Who were you talking to?'"

Elena said, "That soldier."

Mary didn't say anything She thought "I didn't see anybody." Mary wondered why only Elena and she had this conversation/interaction.

As Elena became more agitated, she began to be less coherent. Elena was babbling and there was a general warble of girls.

"Where is he?"

"Where did it go?"

"Do you see him now?"

"What are you talking about?"

I realized the last comment came from my mouth. A friend, Laurie, calmly explained that Elena was speaking Spanish, was talking about someone who had been in the room.

At this point I was mildly surprised. Elena never spoke Spanish to us, not even to teach us the bad words. I looked at her and asked, "What happened?"

She turned a look of frightened fury on me. "There was a man in a cape in here and he had a gun with a bayonet. He was standing right next to me!"

I was stunned. Looking from one person to the other, I said in a small voice, "Maybe it was my dad."

Elena rolled her eyes, "It was not your Dad!" She swore she would never sleep at my house again.

Mary recalls that in the morning she asked Elena about it, and Elena said, "I was talking to my brother" Mary told Elena she was talking in Spanish, which left Elena puzzled, as she thought she was speaking English. We didn't find out what she said. Mary thought she said she was talking to her dead brother. Her brother died as a baby.

Regardless of what happened, Elena never came back out and she would not talk about that night. I couldn't imagine my sister getting someone outside the family involved in a trick and Elena had seemed pretty genuine. Mary swore she didn't have anything to do with it. I wondered, in the back of my mind, when and if I would see something.

I certainly didn't have long to wait.

In winter of that year, we'd gotten in the habit of going to church on Saturday night versus Sunday morning. We never knew if we were going to be able to get out or not to get to church because of all the snow that year. And my mother, being a devote Catholic, couldn't let us skip church for fear we'd burn in Hell itself.

That particular Saturday night, we stopped at Art's pizza, which was a Saturday night tradition (and which today still has some of the best pizza in Indiana). As my mom and sister were unpacking the pizza, I sat down in the fireplace room. I lit some candles, which I thought were so beautiful, and I watched the fire in the fireplace.

Out of the corner of my eye, I saw a white ball of light about two feet across, come down our stairs and stop in front of me. At first I blinked my eyes, thinking I had watched the fire too long. As it hovered and bounced slightly. It suddenly dropped into a figure of a man with a cape. And I knew that he knew that I knew that he knew he was there. I couldn't breath and my time seemed to slow down. I remember hearing Mary in the kitchen, but it seemed really far away, versus just in the next room. I looked at the ghost figure, while my heart thumped in my ears until I thought they would burst. I started to take in the apparition. He was tall, well built and not too slender. He looked like a piece of newsprint in that he was all black with a white outline around buttons, edges of clothing. I could not see his feet. He had naught but black pits for eyes, but I could see the ridge of his nose and the curve of his jaw. Everything on this man really screamed good looking, especially the fact that his hair was long enough to be tied in a queue and I could see the ribbon. He didn't have a gun. My vision changed and I could see he had on a gray cape and his hair was black. The ribbon was blue.

By this time, I had calmed somewhat and while still looking at him, I called to Mary, trying to keep the panic out of my voice. She asked what I wanted and I said, somewhat annoyed, "Just get in here!"

She flopped through the doorway and said, "What do you want?" It was then that I realized she couldn't see him. She was standing two feet from him and she could not see him! I debated about telling her about him versus having her move. But in the time it took me to process that idea, he simply vanished.

When I told my sister what had happened, she freaked out, but we knew to keep it hush-hush, as Mom would have had a fit. When I finished talking, she said, "Look!" and we saw every candle I had lit was now out and wisps of smoke were still coming from the wicks.

After that incident, it seemed to be open season in the house. Mary woke up one night screaming that she saw the devil on the ceiling. She wouldn't go to sleep until both of us fell asleep from sheer exhaustion. Although I didn't see anything, I could feel the terror in her voice. We were always surprised our parents didn't come up and get involved.

Many other odd experiences happened in the house. Lorri, who was undoubtedly the most sensitive and tuned in to what was happening, had many experiences above and beyond what I've written about. Once, when Mary and I were having a sleepover, she came downstairs and asked us if we'd snuck in her room. Of course we said no. Many years later Lorri told us she was really "tripped out" because she was hoping we would have said yes. She said, "I wasn't mad. I really wanted you to say yes because I didn't want the things I saw to be what they were." She told us that night, she saw two children, one of which looked like me with a curly perm, they had shaken her awake and then resumed playing on the floor.

Additionally, one evening Lorri was in bed with Spiecy, one of our many cats. She said he was lying on her tummy and she was reading. She noticed his ears perked up and he looked over in the corner where her bookshelf was and just watched it. "Suddenly, I heard the box with my chess pieces move. It moved like someone was holding it at an angle off the bookshelf and you could hear the pieces moving. Spiecy jumped down and scratched at the door to get out. I just sat there scared and wondering what my next move was going to be."

Lorri said one of the few times she was not upset or scared about what was going on in the house was when she was in the kitchen, looking into the room with the fireplace. Out of the corner of her eye, she caught something move and she stood in the door to have a better look. Moving from east to west, she saw a large pair of men's boots without a body disappear into the wall. I often wondered if these boots were the missing feet for my apparition.

To Lorri though, her most unnerving incident happened as she took care of the ponies we had. Originally, we'd bought one pony for Terri, a friend of Lorri's who had leukemia. Thinking she might die, our mother bought her a pony. Lorri took care of Tonka religiously. Little did we know that the pony was pregnant. One day, Lorri went down about 5:30 a.m. to feed Tonka and there was a baby in the stall with her, later named Shasta.

On this particular morning though, Shasta had long since been born. Our dad used to leave to work at Delco-Remy Remy in the start of its decline in the 1980s, however, Lorri said he was still home. She recalled:

"It was dark and the weather was comfortable. I went to the garage, and let the dog, Ashes, out on his leash. As usual, I walked towards barn. I had it down to the point I hit the same path every day. I got onto the concrete pad next to the silo bases, watching the ground so I didn't trip on the slight lip of the concrete. Once on the concrete, I looked up. The front door of the barn was open and the door (which was really a piece of the metal siding with boards attached), was leaning inside barn. The ponies weren't making any noise. Sometimes they did when they heard me and they would nicker and whine. Looking

at that opening,

I caught movement in far right corner. Something white was standing there, then it was just gone. I backed up and looked hard at the opening. I could hear normal noises, like Ashes scraping around. Whatever it was came out and floated forward.

I was not quite in the fight/flight/freeze mode and I wasn't terrorized, although I was poised to run if the fear level got any higher.

I started to focus on the figure. It was milk white, with t head and edge of shoulders. Where the arms were more transparent. The very bottom about 6-8 inches, was very transparent to the point there were almost no feet. The figure got very straight up and down and started floating forward. It didn't swing any arms back and forth—and there was no depth to figure. As it got to the edge of the barn, before it came out, it stood straight up. It was the shape of an arm and it went down but I couldn't see hands. In the middle of the chest to belly to the groin, the figure became more transparent and by the time you got to where the pants would be, although there were no clothing marks, it was even

I was grateful it wasn't bloody. I thought 'the old man burned in the barn'. I perceived maleness to it. By this time, it got to middle of garden area (about 50 feet away from her) and it got to milk house foundation (about 25 feet away from her), I said, 'Mmm right' and ran back home. I got the red flashlight lantern we always kept near the back door. I grabbed the dog leash, took Ashes with me. He didn't act up or anything. Humming to myself. I went to the edge of water trough to see if anything was in there. I kept pointing the flashlight at my toes.

I went down the old cattle-feeding trough, on the other side of the barn close to the fence, all the time looking around like 'I don't know anything but I am watching out for things'. I went in the barn fast, with the dog leash in one hand, flashlight in the same hand flashing it around. The ponies were at the gate. I talked to them like nothing was there, booked them fast into the pasture. Grabbing the bridles in the other hand, I took a deep breath, put the dog back, and moved at a clip you wouldn't be-lieve. I later found out that where I saw the figure in the barn was where a man had been killed in the original barn when it burned. It was someone from the German Baptist church that had been the former owners."

Lorri wasn't the only one to have experiences outside our shared ones. Mary was 11 or 12 and saw a man that looked like 'the guy in V for Vendetta'. She was in the basement just noising around because "it was something to do." She went towards the part of the basement that was under the old one room schoolhouse. The former owners had used it to store preserves and canned vegetables, however, we didn't store anything there. The room was damp, ill lit and always a little dark. The floor was cement but it looked like a dirt floor because no one wanted to be in the room long. It was never swept clean. The beams for the floor above were hand-hewn logs.

Mary was about to go into the room, when she saw him. His arms were in front of him and he was looking at the shelves, touching them like he was looking for something. He was in a dark "Barnabus Collins cape" that went to the ground. It had an extra cape layer that would have been used as a hood. One of the first things she noticed besides these things was that he was left handed, the same as she was. His sword and sheath were on his right side. She was scared and he must have seen her because he turned around and looked at Mary. She pretended she didn't see him. She noticed, he had on black boots, black pants over them and a black short 1860s top hat. His cape was clasped at top. The figure had a sword and sheath with a belt around his waist. When he turned to face her, she saw he had a black button-up vest. He had black hair that was long and tucked inside his cape. He had a black beard with a upside down handlebar mustache. She said he seemed to be in his 30s. Mary said, "There's nothing there. What are you looking for?" Without a word, he turned his back to her and stood by the shelves in the north west corner with his hands in front of him and his head down. By this time, Mary decided she'd had enough and she turned around, took a couple steps and looked behind her really quick. She repeated this several times till she got to the stairs and then she ran up the stairs and locked the door. Later, after she'd moved out, she was living in Muncie and she saw a black cloaked man behind a furnace who looked exactly like him.

As we got older, we were left alone for longer periods of time. My mom left one day to go shopping about three in the afternoon. My dad was working and Mary was at a friend's house. Lorri was 16 and her friend Terri had her driver's license, so they were preparing for a night out including a sleepover at Terri's.

I honestly don't remember what I was doing, but the electricity went off. Lorri refreshed my memory on what happened. Apparently, I called her and told her that the lights were off and I was hearing "weird noises". We tried to analyze what I might have heard. Our sump pump was electric so that couldn't have been it and I would have recognized it trying to cool down. Additionally, this was before our house had any battery operated alarm clocks, computers or the like. We had one stereo and that was guarded by Mary. Lorri asked her friend if she'd mind coming out to see what was up with me, deciding not to tell her about the weird noises. When she arrived, I was outside, refusing to stay inside. The sun was setting in the early Fall evening and the shadows in the house were getting longer. Lorri called the utilities and they had no reports of any other power outages. We could see lights on at the neighbors to the south and to the east. Shortly after this, Mom came home. She didn't seem too concerned about it or maybe she wanted to avoid the issue.

When my sisters moved out, things didn't quiet down. Several times I would come home and things would be moved or missing. I could dismiss these as my mother snooping through my possessions, however, a few instances I couldn't let go.

One night, I awoke to find myself facing the room none of us liked. It was a room which overlooked the front of the house and which connected the two upstairs bedrooms' closets. The room was fine to be in during the day, but as night came on, it creeped all of us out. In the summer hazy early morning, I found myself watching a hunched over figure rummaging through the writing papers I had out in the room. By this time I was a seasoned veteran. I knew it wasn't my mother and I certainly wasn't going to ask it what it wanted. I simply closed my eyes and fell asleep.

The last experience I had in the house, and one that was most truly frightening happened one Friday night before I went to sleep. My sisters had long since moved out and I was alone upstairs. I was normally a night owl, but found myself extraordinarily tired. Wanting to get a good night's sleep, I started to put things away and get ready to shut the light off. I heard a huge bang on the wall behind my headboard. At first I thought I had somehow jiggled the bed.

Then I heard it.

The scratching on the door.

I couldn't believe I heard it, but it had happened. I knew the bang on the wall was not from my bed. And in the back of my mind, I didn't know why I hadn't heard footsteps. If it had been anyone other than my sisters, they would not have known which steps to choose to come up silently.

I hadn't heard any footsteps.

If it had no tread, could it come through the door?

The slightly loose porcelain doorknob began to turn. Had I locked the door? I looked at the dead bolt and breathed a sigh of relief. Yes, I had.

Insistently, the door began to shake and rattle. Something banged against it.

I couldn't decide whether or not to whip out "in the name of Jesus Christ be gone". I quickly decided on a happy medium and grabbed the small cross from my wall. In what I hoped was a firm voice I commanded, "Stop it!"

The door handle moved a few more times and was silent.

I stayed awake until the light of day and I never heard anyone go back down the stairs.

I moved out in the late 1980s and my parents sold the house shortly after. Since that time, there have only been two owners of the house. I was fortunate enough to be able return to the house and have a tour. The new family has three girls and one boy- all within 2 years of each other in age. The family room is now an office, the fireplace room is now the family room.

Shortly before I moved out and my parents sold the house, they did an even worse 1980s remodel on bits of the house. The plaster walls of the stairway were sparkle spackled. The 10 foot ceilings upstairs now sported ugly drop ceilings. The current owners have made the house a home, including turning the creepy attic into a spacious bathroom. They also used part of that space to make a playroom for the girls.

Originally, I had only wanted to show my husband around the outside- to show him where I had grown up. The owner was so kind and told me she hadn't had the opportunity to tour her old house and if I could ignore the mess, I could look around- and perhaps answer a few questions about the house.

As I walked around the house, it brought back so many memories. The house had largely unchanged in structure and they even had the same curtains that we had inherited up in the reading room.

I answered questions about house structure and why things were done the way they were, but I did not tell the owner about her possible unwanted guests. In 2005 when I returned with Lorri, the owner proudly showed us the new bedroom they'd built for their almost teenage daughter--in the basement. Next to the dark, creepy room.

According to Mary, our father claims today that there were no ghosts in the house. Our mother has never commented.

And what of Father Fennessy? He was sent away shortly after he blessed our house due to severe drug and alcohol problems. Around 1985, he resurfaced at the Bennett High School in Marion, Indiana and as I heard through the grapevine, was later accused of molesting two teenage boys. According to sources close to the issue, he was sent away again. Finally, I was told on Mother's Day 1989, he tied a plastic bag around his head and killed himself, leaving a rather revealing suicide note about his life and relationships within it.

Since writing this story originally in 2006, we've had a chance to talk with the owners of the house about their experiences. They've not seen what we did, however, they have seen two children with schoolbooks in the attic-turned-bathroom upstairs. Additionally, the female owner states that she sees a demon that has followed her since she was six years old. When she encounters it, she prays and it goes away.

Above. This photo was taken inside the barn as part of a multi-part rapid series.

Below. This photo is part of the rapid series grouping and is the only photo with such anomalies. Close ups of certain sections of this picture can be seen on the next few pages.

Left, close up of the man on the right side of the previous picture. No-tice how he is holding his caped arm up.

Right. This is an even closer picture of the man's face. He appears to have his mouth open and has dark hair.

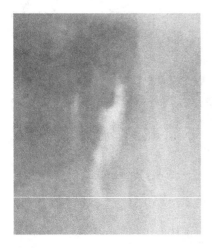

Left, close up of the woman to the left of the man. In this photo, you can see the outline of the right side of her face.

Bottom, this photo is part of the man's cape. The photo to the right is the way it appears untouched and close up.

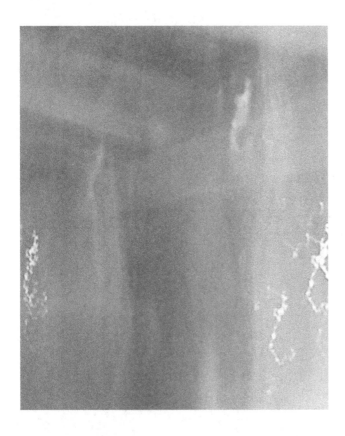

This photo shows three ectoplasmic strings. See close up of the upper left string in the inset at the bottom left of the picture.

Elder House
Alexandria, Indiana

When I went in search of information about the Elder House, I ended up spending a couple of delightful hours at the Alexandria Historical Society. For anyone who hasn't been to any historical society, you're missing out. And Alexandria was exceptional. When you walk in, you're offered a chair- or you're offered a tour. On a tight schedule, we took the chairs and asked questions, but know we will be back very soon.

Part of the reason I love writing so much, especially about ghost and history is that it is like a house with a lot of secret passages. You find a little at a time and eventually you'll understand all of it or bask in the continuing mysteries presented to you. The people you meet along the way are fascinating. Good, bad, or just plain characters, interviewing is a great study in human behavior. In this round of discovery, I got to meet Clifford Leroy "Pete" Sayre, who is a wonderful storyteller. I suppose being in his line of business as a policeman and hearing and seeing it all, that he might have been influenced in that respect. When we spoke of the police and issue they have today, he told us that back in the day, you were expected to do your job as a policeman. As proof, he told us his chief once told him "If you can't take care of it, lay your gun and badge on the counter." Once he retired after 20 years in 1971, he drove a school bus.

He and the others in the room that day told us that unfortunately, they didn't have a lot of information about the home. It was built by Mr. Samuel A. Cook, who was the majority shareholder of the Alexandria Paper Company. His partners, Mr. Yewel and Mr. Lancaster both owned a quarter share. They had the agreement drawn up so that if one should die, the shares would revert to the other shareholders. Not a lot of information exists about Mr. Lancaster.

Mr. Yewel was remembered as a generous man. He lived at the south west corner of Lincoln and John Streets in a beautiful home that still stands and receives love from its owner. Leroy remembered him in several stories. When Leroy was about 5 years old, he met Mr. Yewel, who was a "grand man". He'd come out to Leroy's family farm. His family actually farmed the land for Mr. Yewel. His driver, Gover, drove a Packard. Mr. Yewel asked Leroy if they should go get ice cream. Leroy, who claims to have been shy, was told he could go by his father. Leroy was delighted when Mr. Yewel bought chocolate ice cream. It was the first time Leroy had ever heard of it. He thought he was living large when they rode in the car while eating ice cream.

When Leroy was 12 years old, his father told him to pick any two acres and told him he could grow whatever he wanted on them. So Leroy chose tomatoes. Mr. Yewel would come out and talk to Leroy about how weed free they were. When harvest time came, Leroy, his father and brothers backed them up and took them to the canning factory.

Leroy received a check and his dad took him to the Alexandria Savings and loan to give to Mr. Yewel. They got the money and took it to Mr. Yewel. Mr. Yewel counted it all out, divided the money into two piles, all the while talking about what a good crop "they" had and what a good job "they" did.

He asked Leroy what he was going to do with it and he said he was going to put it in the Commercial Bank, where Yewel was chairman. Mr. Yewel told Leroy he'd enjoyed talking with him about tomatoes so he gave him all the money and put it in the bank. In 1949 Leroy bought a new car and part of this money was used for it.

Mr. Yewel eventually ended up owning the entire mill. Mr. Cook died in 1918.

Mr. Cook had his own story. He was born in Ontario, Canada in 1849. When he was nine, his father moved the family to Stockbridge, Wisconsin. Two years later, his mother, his brother and sister went back to Canada to sell some property. On their way back, they crossed Lake Michigan on the Lady Elgin, and tragically, the mother and daughter died. The $16,000 in gold was claimed by the lake. At 15 years of age, Mr. Cook enlisted in the service during the Civil War. Afterwards, he opened a store and later a paper mill in Menasha, Wisconsin. After 10 years, he sold the mill and opened the Alexandria Paper Company.

In 1894 he was elected to Congress. He was nominated for a Republican candidate for governor and later the Senate. He was the Department Commander of the DAR and was most benevolent. He also gave an armory to the national guared in Menasha and Neenah, Wisconsin. His wives died in 1874 and 1895 and his son, who was manager of the mill died in 1931. His daughter was married to Mr. Charles Lancaster of Boston. He's buried in Oak Hill in Neenah.

He built the house around 1875. He could see the Alexandria Paper Company from his home. For many years, it was his home, his

This undated photo shows the Cook house with the paper mill to the right middle of the picture. (Photo courtesy of the Alexandria Monroe Township Historical Society)

son's. One of the best features of this house is the double sided fire place. We are unsure if this was an original feature or a later addition to the home, but it does make a beautiful focal point.

It passed on to other people. It was known as the Colonnade when teas and special event catering were handled in the house. It was also part of assisted living, which is where its common name, Elder House, was taken from. At one time, it had a doctor or a veterinarian in it. The most recent inhabitants are said to be a military family.

The house is listed with 12 bedrooms, 7 baths and a grand total

Above, Mrs. Cook. (Photo courtesy of the Alexandria Monroe Township Historical Society)

Right, Mr. Cook (Photo from Paper, Volume 22, 1918)

of 22 rooms. It isn't as grand as it used to be on the outside and most of the beautiful trees I remember seeing around it driving by as I was growing up are gone. The house was purported as haunted for many years. As one older gentleman told me, "Everyone thought it was haunted by Mr. Cook after his death." As I grew up, my family drove by the house every couple weeks or so on our way to see my grandparents and we speculated about. It fell into some disrepair when I was a teenager and many people I knew went into the house. They marveled at the beauty, but didn't stay for long usually. Sometimes they would party in the home, but usually got scared out by noises. Sometimes this lack of staying power was attributed to the police, other kids or just the squeaks and creaks of an old house. Local teens began to believe Mr. Cook haunted the house when strange winds would blow hotly through the home.

A group of teenagers in the 1986 ran screaming back to their cars when they felt one such wind accompanied by a "howling screech." Some naysayers believe that it was just the wind whistling through the house, but the teens believe otherwise.

The most significant story comes from George, who just wanted to look around the house. He is in the construction business and doesn't scare easily. "I like history, and as it was empty, it seemed the perfect time." He went through the house with a friend, marveling at how beautiful it was and how much of the original interior remained despite the house changing hands.

"I looked into an ornate square mirror in one of the rooms on the west side. I was surprised it was there and not broken. The frame was beautiful with swirls and flowers on it. The mirror was old and kind of cloudy, but I wasn't alone in it. A man in turn of the century clothing stood next to me smiling. I looked to the left and right and back at him. I took a step closer just to make sure I was really seeing it. The man stayed behind me. Turning around, I still saw nothing.

"Then my buddy came in the room. He was bugging me to take some of the items in the house, and I said no. Then he asked me what I was doing. I told him that Mr. Cook, because that's the feeling I got, was standing with us. My friend looked around and laughed nervously, saying 'I don't see anything.' I told him to look in the mirror."
George laughed. "I never saw him move so fast in my life. I thought he was going to hurt himself, he was tripping over stuff. As he was running towards the door, it started banging back and forth. I don't think the man

liked the idea of his things leaving the house. I looked back into the mirror, and the man was still there. I gave him a nod, told him I liked his house and moved on. "

George believes the man was Mr. Cook looking after his home. The spirit to him was just a part of the house like the mirror. "I wasn't scared because I wasn't there to do anything bad. I wish I could have helped the house in some way, but at the time, I wasn't making a lot of money."

The Cook/Elder House continues to be a source of conversation today. Hopefully, it will remain standing for future generations to enjoy. For me, I can't help but wonder what Mr. Cook thinks of the condition of his house now.

3129 E Lynn Street

Anderson, Indiana

When my ex-husband and I were first married, we had no money. We were working at Meis-Elderbeerman and making a little more than minimum wage, which at the time was about $3.15 per hour. Both of us worked hard. He was a maintenance worker and I worked in the maternity and children's areas.

Our apartment in the old house was the porch section that had been added at some point. It had a large living room, a good sized kitchen and one bedroom. We even had a 1950s refridgerator that had a special shelf for 12 ounce bottles of pop. The bathroom was a ghastly affair with a concrete shower. It was like being at a year-round campground and bleach didn't make it any better.

There was at least one apartment upstairs and a smaller efficiency unit downstairs. Having lived in an old house, the regular bumps and creaks had no affect on me and none on my husband, who did not believe in that sort of thing. But a few times, when I was alone, I sensed things were not right.

Once, I was in our living room and the door to our bathroom closed. I thought perhaps someone had moved upstairs and triggered it. Then I realized the bathroom was still in the back porch area. Several times I saw dark shadows crossing our bedroom door.

The worst was when we'd come home of an evening and I would feel like something was in the apartment. A quick check revealed no one, but a malicious presence seemed to linger.

I guess in my mind at the time, I chalked it up to just bad energy. It was a darker, tight space. The Feng Shui certainly wasn't up to par. Something had happened in the house's history that bled over to our newer section. My then-husband was having none of it.

This was also a few years after I'd had my first paranormal experiences and my awareness and self-awareness was not developed much at this point. Had I understood myself a little better, I would have known that it was all foreshadowing.

To this day, I will feel events coming on. Most times, they are about my family, but sometimes in general, I can sense things that are going to happen. When I get these feelings, it is almost like electricity snapping in the air. It is almost alive and palpable. I often feel like there is truly one thin veil separating me from the event and with more development, I may be able to breech the divide and know more about what is going to occur before it does. For example, this summer, I had a fleeting thought that the mother of a friend was going to die. Two weeks later, she did.

It was 1988 and I was trying to go back to school- and failing miserably. Ironically enough, an Achilles heel of mine at Purdue was the World Literature class and it wasn't any better at Ball State. Later, I took a CLEP exam, passed, and got the hell out of the class. To this day, I hate "Beowulf" and dislike professors who believe the common themes are the only themes in a story.

I had a whole day off to go back through a failed test paper and rewrite it for partial credit. I was determined to do well. Best laid plans.

For a time, I was immersed in Beowulf until the couple above us started arguing. For an old house, it certainly had thin walls. The fighting I could stand. The rape I couldn't. The Anderson Police told me, "That's just a domestic disturbance." And with that, another violent crime against a woman went unchecked.

By this time, it escalated and I was terrified. There was no evidence he would come after me. I called the police again after it sounded like he was killing her. Again, I was told that it was a domestic disturbance and they wouldn't come out. I asked them how they could stand by and let someone be physically hurt (at the very least). They asked me if I had actually seen the physical damage. When I said no, they said there was nothing they could do. To this day, I am outraged at this blatant lack of regard. One can say, "oh that was the way it was back in the day." I call bullshit.

Needless to say, when my (now ex) husband came home, I was in tatters. The girl moved out shortly after. I do not know what became of either of them.

I am convinced that there was something hateful lurking in the house, leftover from another era or perhaps with my recent unfriendly departure from my parents and the emotions surrounding me, something attached to me inside or outside the house. Perhaps the couple above were a product of their own hell. Perhaps not. When they first moved in, they were very happy sounding (thin walls), although things change.

The house was miserable and unhappy,. I was glad we moved out. into another house covered in this book on West Sixth Street.

The house always had an uneasy feeling. Darkness still lurks at this house, even during the daylight hours.

The Unhappy Spaniard
E 600 N, Summitville, Indiana

The woman peered out the window. They were coming back. They always did. But this time it was different. Her worried hands smoothed the front of her red and black gown. Well, let's see how many of them see me today, she thought. Her heels made an invisible tap as she went down the stairs in a cool breeze, just in time to see the door open and the first person peek his head in…….

The Second Empire house is a treat for the senses. In the early 1980s, it sat on five acres. It is a brick home with a three storey tower, most likely used for ventilation. The narrow side porch still clung to its ornate woodwork. Inside, it had no bathrooms, no discernible gas connection and certainly no electricity. Looking into the kitchen, it contained a hand pump and large country kitchen sink. If one stepped out the back, you could see an old motor above the back door with bad wiring Perhaps there was some electricity outside after all. The old walls were grey and peeling. Nothing in the house indicated that the roof was anything but sturdy.

When you stepped into the hall, you could see there were no stairs to get to the tower but it looked enticing to view the third floor had a set to the tip top of the tower. Dark, oak woodwork on the floors, walls and staircase gleamed weakly in the faltering light.

The outbuildings included a garage, milk house, smoke house and barn. The milkhouse contained several long, hinged boxes on both sides of the aisleway. Perhaps these were for ice. At the end of the building was an enamel trough with a faucet. The smokehouse had a simple fire pit in the middle and numerous hooks to hang meat from. The small hay barn was in need of repair.

The day Lorri went, many people were milling about. The house was for sale for a pretty good price. She and her ex-husband, Ira were interested in the property because of its history and the land. They could do a lot with it. Bring in horses. Plant a garden for their needs. She said they never got the house because they were outbid. But she did say the house had an occupant that time forgot.

When Lorri was about to go upstairs, she heard the click of a heel on the floor and heard a swish of petticoat meets silk. A blond woman was wearing an 1860s looking red dress with black embroidery.

It had three quarter length sleeves. She had a snood in the same color encasing her hair bun that went down to her shoulders. She wore black lace up boots. Lorri got the impression she was upset so many people were walking through her house.

The House on Parker Hill

Pendleton, Indiana

The Old Kinnard House sits on Parker Hill, a beautiful reminder of a time long passed. But it is none the less pretty. While the exact date of construction is fuzzy, we do know that Colonel George Parker and his wife, Margaret built it. One version of his life story states that the couple was childless. Other accounts state he had two boys, one "brought him shame" and the other (named Fred) "did him proud."

Col. Parker was a Civil War veteran and the 13 child from a Jewish family from Kentucky. After the Civil War, he came north, saw this beautiful hill, and bought the land. The limestone for the foundation came from a quarry on Fall Creek. The pine woodwork was brought from northern Michigan. Huge mirrors in the front rooms came from France, sailed to New Orleans and brought on flatcars to Indiana. The beautiful staircase is made of ash and walnut.

And they say that the burial spot of Col. Parker's beloved war horse is in back of where the carriage house stood. The horse was supposedly buried standing up.

They lived there till about 1918, the Colonial's death and then Hortense and Morris Kinnard bought it in 1920. The Kinnards loved history and spending time with children. Hortense would often pass warm cherry pies to the children of her neighbors.

In the 1980s, this warmness was long gone. People used to sneak into the old house. My sister Lorri was no exception. She used to sneak in the summer kitchen window later in the evening. They would park by the falls and boost people in through the window. At the time they went through, "it was full of junk, dark, and creepy.."
She also heard noises that didn't "seem natural." It was "a tapping that didn't come from woodpeckers." She said they would hear a tap, tap, then it would stop and they would hear fabric like "skirts rustling" close by.

But they never saw anything.

Another time she went with her ex-husband, Ira; my other sister, Mary; and a friend, John. They talked about ghosts and such for a while. Lorri moved her sitting area from one chair to another to get comfortable. Mary said she had nightmares about the house. Suddenly, the old fashioned brass ashtray scooted from one end of the table to the other. Mary and John were nonplussed by this activity. Lorri was "freaked out, as my mediumship was not developed at that point." Ira thought the devil was in the house and wanted to leave.

Not really ready to leave, they convinced Ira to stay. Then they decided to get away from the area and roam the house. Lorri and Ira went to one of the windows on the first floor near the entry way and stairs. They both heard a loud boom upstairs. "It was like something heavy and hard dropped," Lorri said, but nothing reverberated downstairs and no dust moved. Lorri verified that Mary and John were still downstairs.

Ira wanted to go check it out, ready for a fight by this point. He could deal with the living, it seemed, just not the dead. They went up and nothing was out of place or disturbed. In the area, there were some built in cupboards, but nothing in them. They could not find the source of the noise.

They visited the house several times. During one visit, Mary said she looked out the window and the daffodils in front of the house withered and died in front of her eyes. Once, when Lorri and Ira went back during the day, the inside was really dark because the widows had been shuttered from the inside. They found the stairway had been boarded over and the front doorway inside had been crisscrossed with boards nailed to it. Disregarding them, they went to the room at the top of the stairs. It was relatively plain with beadboard and wainscoting. Inside the room, they found Victorian clothes- hats, puffed sleeved blouses, and shirts. Both of them got a bad vibe as though someone had been killed or died in the room.

At the time, some of the original gas fixtures were still in the house. There were fireplaces throughout the house with various types of décor including Art Nouveau and earlier Victorian gilt framed mirrors. Off the east parlor, there was an bedroom. The impression Lorri got from it was that an old woman died there. To the left on the south wall, there was a strange cubby room that had been made into a half bath. The entry hall had a huge deer head in it.

On the west side, there was a matching parlor with stairs to the landing. If you went to the landing and went upstairs, you were treated to a group of rooms that opened into each other. If you stayed in the room, you'd see a creepy little bathroom on the west wall that contained a claw foot bathtub and sink, full of stinking black, slimy water that screamed bad things happened. From this room, you could go to the

The House on Parker Hill.

porch, dining room or kitchen. The area was beautiful with pocket doors, and in storage were glass globes for older lights. They also say a clay sculpture of a woman on her back. And a statue of a hula dancer with red hair.

On this particular visit, Ira was in love with the deer head and he wanted to take it with him. But they couldn't get it down off the 15 foot tall wall. Ira went on to look at something else, and Lorri noticed a gentleman who reminded her of the "KFC dude". He had a dark suit with a white shirt and a string tie. His face was narrow, she said, and clean shaven. "He was tapping his way down the stairs with his cane." He stared at her with "rheumy looking" ice blue eyes and disappeared toward the bottom of the stairs. She was so taken aback, she asked Ira to see if he saw anything and he said he found nothing.
They left and came back that night. When they arrived, they climbed back in their usual window. Imagine their surprise when the cane that the man was using was at in the kitchen leaning against the a stairway that was blocked by debris and wood. She took it home until she divorced and said she never had any problems from it.

The basement walls were dirt and collapsing although it did have fireplaces. Lorri literally rolled into the basement from a gap between the grass and the side of the house. When she stood, Lorri came face to face with a white wispy apparition of a girl in a pinafore dress standing next to a fireplace. "She was ragged around the edges and she seemed to float and sway. The girl stood there a few seconds and then disappeared."

Over time, the house was bought and rejuvenated. Today it looks as beautiful as ever– the house on Parker Hill.

Booco, Bocco, Bucco Cemetery
*West side of CR 100E, between CR 350 S and CR 400 S,
Anderson, Indiana*

Issac Booco's grave is a reminder of a man who was the first land owner in Anderson Township and a man who donated the half acre where it rests for a family and neighbor cemetery.

But this isn't his whole story. He was a hard man prone to rages, especially when it seemed someone was taunting him or making him look unfavorable. His family ended up in the courts to settle problems within the family. His oldest son, William seemed to be the bane of his life. According to Issac, William gave him lots of trouble. His father went to far as to call William a "natural born damned fool" and a "damned mean scoundrel."

The deputy sheriff put a lien on some property that Booco owed money on. Additionally, he put the property up for sale. Booco exercised his rights and protested in front of the courthouse shouting that the sheriff's department was a bunch of "damned malfeasers."

It seemed even when he was sick, he was a bit of a whiner. He called his friend, Issac Clem, over to write his will once when he was ill. His friend dutifully took down his words, which included excluding William and giving everything to the rest of the family. Clem then asked, "Aren't you going to give Shake Stanley your wind pipe for a flute?"

Booco jumped out of bed and went after Clem, who escaped. Booco recovered fully and lived a long time.

Apparently, Booco was also a good hunter and once while on a coon hunt he asked the boys with him to settle down because they "scare the coons.". They stopped laughing and cutting up but soon started again. Booco yelled, "Don't you know that a coon is a hell of a sly thing?" The boys laughed loudly this time, for if there were any coons around, Booco had done a far greater job of scaring them away with his voice.

Issac Booco isn't the only character in this cemetery. Daniel Hoppes was killed by Milton White over the theft of meat. When Hoppes confronted White, they walked back to his farm to search it. On the way, they were seen by several people which made the collar very easy. Hoppes was found with a skull fracture covering the right side of his head. His head and face were crushed so badly they melted into the ground. A club made of sassafras was found nearby with bone, hair and blood clotted on it.

Hoppes was a quiet man who kept largely to himself. Everyone said if White had returned the meat to Hoppes, they were sure that would have been all that was made of it.

White was tried, convicted and sentenced to death. One the night before his death, he was a bit like a caged tiger. The press received very little cooperation for interviews and he mostly glared at them "which was calculated to make one's blood run cold."

The hanging itself was a large affair with a large crowd and a carnival like atmosphere. Father Crawley intoned the Lord's Prayer with White at the gallows. White's voice was "clear and distinct, without the slightest suspicion of tremor."

Finally, the cap was put over his head, the noose drawn, and the cord cut. White's body made a ghastly thud, making the beam holding him shudder. White was forever still.

One has to wonder if these characters are still hanging around the cemetery. Some ghost hunters believe they are. Cassie and Josey consider themselves "independent paranormal investigators." They shun groups and prefer to work alone. While doing a daytime walk-though of the cemetery, Cassie got the surprise of her life. "I was simply walking the small cemetery checking for any obstructions or issues that might make for bad night time adventures. I'd just made the comment that the cemetery looked unkempt and started making fun of myself for not being able to pronounce the name of it. An unseen hand grabbed my ankle so hard, I heard the slap of skin on skin. I looked down, at first thinking it was a vine, but nothing was there. The hand tightened and I screamed for Josey. "

Josey continued, "I saw her struggling. Cassie fell down and was literally being dragged backwards. I ran over to her and she screamed, 'it has my ankle!' I pulled her arms but that didn't work. I tried pulling her ankle and that didn't work. Finally in desperation, I said, 'Issac, leave her alone!' Cassie stopped moving."

"I was shaking the whole time but when do you get an opportunity like this?"

I fully believe Issac was at fault here. In the afterlife, people are usually in death as they were in life. Issac was cantankerous to say the least. We're looking forward to our next trip to the cemetery to experience the paranormal and to see the progress on the cemetery.

SPIRITED SHORTS

This section contains many stories that have been unable to be investigated, or that are in the process of investigation. Too short to include separately, but part of Madison County's haunted history nonetheless.

Enjoy!

Old Anderson High School

Anderson has always been a basketball town and the fans are incredible. I have happy memories myself as a teenager playing basketball and attending basketball games. I loved half time when the percussion section of Madison Heights would play "no see" (some kids nick named it Nazi). The pounding drums and the cheering of the students really rallied everyone.

Anderson High School has longevity and many locations. The first school was organized in 1873 and the students attended classes in various homes and churches. Later they met in the opera house until a building on Main Street was built. Later the school moved to Lincoln School on 12th Street and in 1889 the first school was built at Lincoln and Twelfth Streets.

Eventually the school grew. In 1910 the Manual Arts and Domestic Sciences Building was built between Lincoln and Thirteen and Fourteenth Streets. In addition to shop and home economics facilities, it had an auditorium and swimming pool. In 1925 a new gym was built but it was destroyed by fire in 1958. Finally, the iconic Wigwam opened in 1961, which housed the gymnasium, cafeteria and Olympic sized pool.

By the 1970s, prosperity enveloped Anderson and the school as well as two others, Madison Heights and Highland boasted close to 2000 students. Anderson High School was expanded in the 1970s and for the first time, classes were held under one roof. But all good things must come to an end.

In the 1990s many companies had closed, pulled out of Anderson and had downsized employees. Faced with money shortages, Madison Heights was closed and Anderson High School was moved from Lincoln Street to Madison Ave. The old school was to be used for senior citizen apartments, but on June 25, 1999 a fire destroyed the building. The Wigwam remained open for school and community events until March 8, 2011 including a historic visit by Hillary Clinton.

The Wigwam remained open until 2011. The cause of the closure was due to money. By closing the building the school system saved $700,000 for 2012. Now, the building that once housed some of the best basketball ever, the building that Andersonians were able to see Hilary Clinton speak in during her 2008 election campaign stands empty.

As the legend has it, a young teenager was raped and killed and her screams are still heard. (I've not found any proof of this.) The old part of the school on the second floor had a ghost that will throw things at you. This ghost seems to have moved to the Wig-Wam area. When Hillary Clinton spoke at the building, several women in the WigWam's restroom reported several rolls of paper towels being thrown and crashing into the wall.

Anderson High School
4610 Madison Ave.

A teenage girl from the 1960s killed herself when she found that a boy she liked wasn't going to take her to a dance as promised. She is seen hanging in the old auditorium (now classrooms) and she walks through the new part of the school (formerly parrt of the outdoor area).

(Note: Anderson High School was originally located by the WigWam on Lincoln St. In the 1990s, Anderson High School was relocated in the Madison Heights High School on the south side of Anderson. Long live the MHHS Pirates! You may have jackhammered our beloved mascot but Pirates never die!)

Greenbriar Addition

In the Greenbriar addition, a legend that's been around since I was a child was that Greta, a spirit of a young girl, roams the area. She supposedly died in a car accident. She will play jokes on people or throw leaves, sticks and other items at people near her.

Dickey Road
Anderson, Indiana

This location is not to be confused with Dickey Cemetery located in the northern part of Madison County. For as long as I can remember, the railroad tracks on this road have long been a source of legend. Even before Anderson Memorial Park Cemetery was established, a misty, dark apparition of a funeral procession is seen near the railroad tracks heading south to north.

Interestingly, the crossing was recently replaced (making the ride across the tracks much less bumpy). I doubt this deters the procession from their destination, whether a cemetery long gone or another home.

Grand Avenue and Huffman Court
Anderson, Indiana

These two roads seem to be a hot bed of activity. Huffman Court is next to a backwater swamp just off white river. An empty field had to be crossed before reaching the backwater, which was home to many frog species, a very large golden carp, and several kinds of water birds. If you followed the edge of the backwater you will come to an old abandoned train trestle. Near the trestle are the ruins of a small house and tiny barn.

An old woman used to live here with her pony. She used the pony to haul firewood in a small cart and to go to and from a local store. The pony eventually died and was buried in the yard of the house where the old woman put a granite marker.

Today you can hear the ghost train clacking down the trestle as well as hear the locomotive's sharp whistle. The old lady is said to be roaming the property sometimes crying and grieving the loss of her pony. Occasionally she will throw pebbles at intruders when she prefers to be left alone.

French Cemetery
Frankton, Indiana

In 1917 a Madison County woman, May Berry, a Red Cross, was the first American woman to die on foreign soil during the war. She is seen walking through the cemetery and sitting under a number of trees within the cemetery. She is wearing a dress with a white apron over it. Today, the Frankton American Legion May Berry Post 469 remains a tribute to her.

Sigler Cemetery
Frankton, Indiana

The cemetery is a beautiful example of a county cemetery on a rolling set of hills. Sadly, some of the stones are in sad disrepair. The cemetery sits at the end for the road across from some abandoned homes. The Sigler family started the cemetery. Jacob Sigler owned the land where Frankton is now. Frankton was named for Francis "Frank" Sigler who designed and developed it.

Strange orbs fly through the cemetery during the day and evening. The mysterious "strands" of lights are also seen by visitors. These lights seem to be shimmering strands of ectoplasm in various colors (blue, red and orange have been reported).

When Michael and I visited the cemetery, we saw many apparitions of children and young women darting around the headstones.

Grovelawn Cemetery
Pendleton, Indiana

As part of a larger cemetery that maintains the old stones, this cemetery boasts some of the oldest settler burials in the county. Fairies and will o' the wisp are seen darting about the old stones. A psychic who visited in 2010 stated that the settlers were at unrest because of the direction Pendleton was taking.

Falls Park

Pendleton, Indiana

John Rogers built his home near the falls of Fall Creek in December 1818. It was a good location and soon, other people followed. Being so near the water, it gave the settlers an advantage- drinking water and power for mills. As the town progressed, a log cabin used as a government building was built nearby. In 1825 Thomas Pendleton moved to the Falls and platted the town, calling it Pendleton.

Although Pendleton is still seen as a sleepy community by some, it has had its share of history. In 1843 Fredrick Douglas spoke in Pendleton. His life was in danger from anti-abolitionist people. Through members of the towns of Pendleton and Westfield, he was taken to Hamilton County to hide for a while. (Westfield was known as pro-abolitionist by slave catchers.)

In 1824 a Native American family was killed by five white men. Four of the men were charged and three were hanged just to the north of the falls. It was the first time white people received capitol punishment for the murder of Native Americans. A plaque commemorates the place where the hanging took place.

Today, eyewitnesses claim that they hear the men swinging in the wind. EVPs of distressed men crying "No, No!" have also been captured.

This historic park is also home to two residual hauntings. Rachel Harris fell into the creek while being chased by her lover John. She was most likely killed instantly from a blow to the head with the rocks around the falls. John dove in after her only to be pulled down by her lifeless body. The residual haunting of this event is reenacted in the early mornings, usually around 7:15-8:00 a.m.

The spot where Rachel and John met their watery, icy end.

Theater Row
Anderson, Indiana

Theater Row is the nickname for Meridian Street. In addition to the Rivera, the State and the Paramount Theaters that I grew up with on that street, it had many others. Some of them are the Cozy, the Starland, the Star, the Princess, the Royal, the Nickeldeon, and the Meridian.

Now, only the Paramount survives as an operating theater which also includes concerts and rental for events. The State Theater is still standing, but only as a vacant building.

Paramount Theatre
1124 Meridian St.

Originally opened August 20, 1929, this glorious theater is one of the two "atmospheric" theaters remaining in the United States. The ceiling is a veritable panorama of twinkling stars and clouds as the lights dim. In full light visitors are treated to a Moorish courtyard effect. This majestic theater contains one of only three Grand Page Theater Pipe organs left in the United States. Throughout the 1970-80s, this theater deteriorated and after a lengthy restoration, it reopened in 1995.

Today, brilliant art work and decorations aren't the only items gracing the theater. In the dressing rooms, a woman dressed in heavy stage makeup is seen primping in a corset and likes to slam doors. A man with a broom walks on the stage and appears in the orchestra pit. The upper balcony is haunted by two mischievous boys who have been caught throwing items into the seats below. A man in the projection room likes to make noises as if he's changing or running a film.

State Theatre
1303-1316 Meridian St.

Sadly unused, this former theater was built in the 1920s and was home to stage and screen stars. In the 1960s Anderson's downtown went downhill and took this theater with it. For a time in the late 90s, it operated as a live venue, but seems to have gone belly up with the rest of the town.

From at least the 1960s, the balcony of the movie theater was haunted by a man in a suit. He was known to sit down next to movie goers and scare them by disappearing into thin air. Later, when the balcony was closed due to safety issues, the man seems to have moved to the main seating area. After the theater closed, many patrons during the 90s claimed to have seen him in the upper restroom areas. Workers also saw the man backstage.

The State theater a few years ago and still empty. The area on the front where the name of the feature displays is no longer completely intact and the building is sadly forlorn.

Old Walmart
1804 S Scatterfield Rd

Although Walmart moved to a new location, the old Walmart building is haunted. From the time Walmart opened, employees swore they heard odd noises.

Sheila used to work the evening shift. Restocking was a priority. One evening, she asked to be moved after her experience. She was stacking boxes when two aisles over stuffed animals and other toys started flying. Several came over the wall and hit her. At first, she thought someone was playing so she said, "Ok, guys. Enough is enough." It stopped for a while and started again. She went around the side to surprise whoever it was and she found no one there. But all the stuffed animals were off the shelf. She picked them up, put them back and went back to her task.

The same thing started. When she went over, annoyed, she was surprised to see the animals "just flying" from the shelves.

Jason used to work in the toy area as well. He'd heard stories from other people, but he witnessed dump trucks rocking back and forth in the aisle as if someone were loading and unloading them.
One time, about 2am, he had a group of three dump trucks follow him throughout the store. "At first, they rolled. Then I asked to be moved and they would just appear wherever I was at that night. It was really creepy.

Other employees swear that the store was haunted by something bad. One employee was sprayed with glass when a whole section of glass bowls fell and shattered. Another woman was sprayed with shards of glass when candles fell.

Chesterfield Christian Church
Chesterfield, Indiana

This church was founded in 1897 by Emory Clifford and Joseph Seward. Until January 1925, the church members met in a building purchased from a Methodist Church. The members sold bricks to raise the money and materials to build the church at Elm and Water Streets.

Unfortunately, the church had difficulties sustaining itself and despite help from area churches, it closed the doors in 1936. However, fate intervened and in 1938 using student pastors from Butler University, the church began again. In 1940 Reverend John Osberg was the first full-time pastor. Many years and many pastors later in 1957, the church was sold and a new church was built at its current location.
Today, the church is a vibrant part of Chesterfield, running concerts and events for the parish and public. Missions are conducted regularly to help others in need. Bible study and classes are a routine part of education and worship.

Despite this glorious gift, the church has its issues. A man was found dead in the boiler room in the 1940s. His death was never solved. Today lights flicker off and on and doors open and close by unseen hands. Mysterious handprints on windows and mirrors appear without cause.

Union Building
SE corner of Meridian and 11th Streets, Anderson, Indiana

Originally built as a department store, it was later changed to house offices. In one of the early law offices, a secretary who stayed late on Friday to work on some letters was killed by an irate client, who cut her throat. She was not found until Monday morning by one of the attorneys.

People have seen this woman dressed in 1940s clothing walking though the offices and spaces that now occupy the building. Additionally, a residual haunting of the act. Many visitors have claimed to have heard her scream and drop to the ground in the early evening.

Fifth Street at Meridian Street
South east corner, Anderson, Indiana

A house at Meridian and Fifth Street was supposedly haunted. In the 1870s, two families lived in the house and swore it was haunted due to the rapping and tapping. Later, a servant admitted she'd engineered the whole thing, showing the wire that was used to make the knocking apparatus work.

Still, people didn't believe that and the house ended up in disrepair. A gentleman went in to prove it wasn't haunted. He screamed, "If you are a spirit, speak to me!" His candle flame flickered, the room became cold, and he heard three knocks.

Running from the house, he never returned again.

Elena's House
Parking lot south of 1420 Broadway Street, Anderson, Indiana

My sister Mary said our friend Elena's house always freaked her out. If I were honest, I would admit that going up the stairs scared me as well. It was an old farmhouse that had been remodeled at different points. When you came in the back door, a cozy kitchen greeted you. It seemed Elena's mother was always in the kitchen cooking and her dad was always puttering around the house or spending time with her mother.

From the kitchen you could see into the living/dining room straight ahead. To the right was a hallway ending with a bedroom and a stairway that went up a few steps, turned and went up several more. It was that turn that always bothered me. I always thought something might be there to greet me.

But this thought never stopped me from going to their house.

Elena's sister, Judy confirmed later that on that landing, the face of a devil would appear. Her father used to pray and wish it away. His thought was if you prayed it wouldn't hurt you.

The house is no longer standing, long since made into a parking lot. Next door is a social services organization in an old church. Outside, next to the parking lot, children play innocently.

North County Road 550 West
Alexandria, Indiana

Three girls were killed on this short stretch of road. They had a cat with them. It is believed as the driver rounded the curve that the cat got in the way and forced her off the road. One of the girls lasted 6 months before she died. She never talked about what happened.

Today, the ghost of the car is seen in on the road.

One witness, Shannon, said that she was driving northbound and a car seemed to come up very quickly behind her. She checked her speed and saw she was going the speed limit, so she thought if they wanted to pass her they could. Suddenly, she saw them kilter out of control and crash to the side of the road. Shannon slammed on her brakes and got out of the car, ready to call the police.

"I ran back to where I saw them go off the road. There wasn't anything there but brush. No car, no people. I know what I heard. Then I realized that it was very quiet and isolated. I got back in my car and went home, leaving all the lights blazing. I didn't sleep that night."

Park Place Elementary School
802 E 5th St Anderson, Indiana

Several staff members from teachers, custodians and lunch ladies claim a woman who looks like she stepped out of the 1970s haunts the school. They all report her walking past them and into classrooms but never speaking with them. When they go to find her, no one is in the room.

Additionally, staff heard random footsteps early in the morning and later in the evening when everyone was gone. One teacher who stayed after an evening event heard someone with keys opening and closing doors very loudly. When she went out to investigate, no one was there.

Florida Station
Florida Station, Indiana

Mrs. Alvin Vineyard had been shopping on April 6, 1894 . She was going across the track coming from behind a building and did not see the train. She was thrown and instantly killed. Was also known as Clark's Station and Keller's Station.

Her figure has been seen from time to time on the anniversary of her death from 1895 to present day. She is seen walking across the tracks and a thump is heard. Some people report seeing her fly as she's hit by the ghost train.

This is the area in which Mrs. Alvin Vineyard was struck by a train and killed. The area to the left is a Native American burial ground according to legend.

Camp Kikthawenund
Frankton, Indiana

As the name suggests, the camp takes its name from Chief Anderson's Native American name. During the summer, the Boy Scouts of America use the facility for a variety of camps and activities. The rest of the year, it can be rented for parties and such. It has several campsites, dining facilities, a lake for canoeing, space for archery and guns, swimming and some lodging.

People who have been to this location report ghost children wondering the 230 acre facility, especially around the dining hall and camp sites. Native Americans are also seen throughout the woods. Many people report seeing strange figures and hearing unexplained noises.

The reason for some of these hauntings could be because the Pipe Creek Trade Station, a nightly stopping point for the stage coach that ran through Madison County, was overtaken by Native Americans. Whites and Native Americans were slaughtered. They say when the moon is full and it is very still, you can hear the horses hooves, hear the jangle of the stage coach, and hear the pitiful screams of the dying.

Another reason may be the legend of Chief Tomalapus. He was killed by a jealous man. The chief was living with a white family who considered him one of their best friends. One interesting feature of the Chief was that he had a five pointed star on his forehead as a symbol of being of warrior class.

A stranger came around and seeing this interaction put him in a state of rage. He killed the chief at the next available opportunity. His friends buried him under a cottonwood, to mark his grave.

According to some boy scouts, the tree is still there, close to the dining hall. For every bad thing that happens on site, the cottonwood gets a little closer to the dining hall. Each branch has a perfect five point star in the middle of each branch. The tree positions itself at night into the shape of Tomalapus, waiting for the unsuspecting.

One Mile House

Anderson, Indiana

One of the oldest structures that remained the longest in Anderson history is the One Mile House. It was located on the north side of West Eighth Street, one mile west of the court house. The plot of land just to the east of John Street by the railroad tracks is the approximate location of the cabin (or for anyone who was told, it was on the spot where the Bliven's gravel pit was).

It was built in 1839 by David Harris' widow for the purpose of being a tavern. It was well known throughout the country. According to some accounts, Eighth Street at that time in the summer was a "continuous stream of covered wagons."

A post stood behind the house where Native Americans would burn their prisoners. Before David Harris came to the area, a French trader killed a Native American woman. He was burned at this stake.

To this day, they say that on an Indian Summer night, the ghost of the Frenchman who was burned alive appears. He is seen with one leg burned off above the ankle, with fierce eyes and blue flames issuing from his nose. Children would not venture into the area after dark for a long time after hearing the story.

Michael and I plan on going out one Indian summer night. Any takers?

The space to the left behind the fence in the park is where the stake was. This stake held the bodies of many including a Frenchman who killed a Native American woman. His ghost roams the area.

References

Anderson Weekly Herald. "Ghost Story". Anderson Weekly Herald. 23 Mar 1900. Print.

Baker, S. (n.d.). Hays Cemetery. In HANCOCK COUNTY, INDIANA, Cemetery Records. (pp. 95-105).

Beck, E. (2006). Personal Interview. Anderson, Indiana.

Beth. Personal Interview. Anderson, Indiana.

Blake-Ferguson, T. (2013 May). Personal Interview. Anderson, Indiana.

Brad. (2013 May). Personal Interview. Anderson, Indiana.

Brunt, J.R. "Pioneer Ways in Pioneer Days". Anderson Herald. 11 Oct 1925. Print.

Cagley, D. (2013 May). Personal Interview. Telephone Interview. Anderson, Indiana.

Carbo, Connie (2013 March). Personal Interview. Telephone Interview. Anderson, Indiana.

Charles. (2013 May). Personal Interview. Anderson, Indiana.

Clifford, R. (1994). "There is a Corner of Madison County that is Haunted by Love." Madison County Magazine. July 1994. Print.

Department of Natural Resources (2011). Mounds State Park Interpretive Master Plan 2011.
Retrieved May 2, 2013 from http://www.in.gov/dnr/parklake/files/
sp-
Mounds_State_Park_IMP_2011.pdf

Department of Natural Resources (n.d.). Ground Water in Indiana. Retrieved May 2, 2013 from http://www.in.gov/dnr/water/files/GroundWaterInIN.pdf

Elwoodindiana.org. (2013, May 31). 31 May 2013 [May 31, 2013 message]. Message posted to http://www.elwoodindiana.org/content/black-history-elwood-opera-house

Elwood Opera House. (n.d.) History. Retrieved May 2, 2013 from http://elwoodoperahouse.com/node/2

Everett, B. & Everett, S. (2013 May). Personal Interview. Anderson, Indiana.

Ferguson, T. & Ferguson, P. (2013 May). Personal Interview. Anderson, Indiana.

Forkner, J. L. (1970). History of Madison County Indiana (Vol. One). Chicago: The Lewis Publishing Company. (Original work published 1914)

Forkner, J.L & Dyson, B.H (1897). Historical Sketches and Reminiscences of

Madison County, Indiana (Vol. One & Two). Logansport, IN: Wilson, Humphreys & Co.)

Fraternal Order of Eagles (2011). Fraternal Order of Eagles Facts. Retrieved May 2, 2013 from http://www.foe.com/about-us/facts.aspx

George (2013 July). Personal Interview. Telephone Interview. Anderson, Indiana.

Gerald (2013 May). Personal Interview. Telephone Interview. Anderson, Indiana.

Green, C. (2013). If You Grew Up in Anderson, IN. Retrieved July 3, 2013 from https://www.facebook.com/groups/249146618437655/permalink/620681554617491/

Green (Baker), M (2013). If You Grew Up in Anderson, IN. Retrieved July 3, 2013 from https://www.facebook.com/groups/249146618437655/permalink/620681554617491/

Gruenewald Home. (n.d.). A Brief Chronology of the Gruenewald Historic House & Site. Retrieved May 2, 2013 from http://gruenewaldhouse.net/chronology.php

Gruenewald Home. (n.d.). The Gruenewald Historic House. Retrieved May 2, 2013 from http://gruenewaldhouse.net/chronology.php

Harlow, K. (2002). Hays Cemetery. In American Ghost Society. Retrieved March 25, 2004, from http://www.prairieghosts.com/hays_cem.html

Hall, R. (2013 May). Personal Interview. Telephone Interview. Elwood, Indiana.

Hartman, S. (n.d.) Original Inhabitants Leave Legacy of Names. Retrieved May 2, 2013, from http://www.andersonmchs.com/indian-names.php

Haunted places in Indiana. (1998). The Shadowlands. Retrieved January 9, 2002, from
http://www.theshadowlands.net/places/indiana.htm

Hawking, Stephen (n.d.) Space and Time Warps. Retrieved May 2, 2013 from http://www.hawking.org.uk/space-and-time-warps.html

Hall, R. (2013). Personal Interview. Telephone Interview, Indiana

Harden, S. (1874). "History of Madison County , Indiana from 1820 to 1874". (Markleville, IN: Harden).

Hays Cemetery (2005). INPCRC Cemetery Hall of Shame. Retrieved May 23, 2002 from
http://www.rootsweb.com/~inpcrp/HallofShame/hayscem.html

Hayes, M.D. (2006). Shadyside Park: Beautiful and full of history. Retrieved May 2, 2013 from http://heraldbulletin.com/peopleandplaces/x518761651/Shadyside-Park-Beautiful-and-full-of-history/print

Indiana Historical Society (n.d.). Saint John's Health System. Retrieved May 2, 2013 from http://www.indianahistory.org/our-services/books-publications/hbr/st-johns-health.pdf

Jackson, S. (2009). Our History: Killbuck tied to missions, role as war chief. Retrieved May 2, 2013 from http://heraldbulletin.com/home-news/x518854049/Our-History-Killbuck-tied-to-missions-role-as-war-chief

Jake, (2002, December). Personal Interviews. Anderson, Indiana.

Jane. (2013 June). Personal Interview. Anderson, Indiana.

Janice. (2013 May). Personal Interview. Anderson, Indiana.

Jason. (2013 May). Personal Interview. Indianapolis, Indiana.

John, (2013, May). Personal Interviews. Anderson, Indiana.

Josey, (2013, July). Personal Interviews. Anderson, Indiana.

Judy. (2013 May). Personal Interview. Anderson, Indiana.

Karen. (2013 May). Personal Interview. Anderson, Indiana.

Keene, M. Lamar. (1997). The Psychic Mafia (Amherst, NY: Prometheus).

Kirkwood, D. (2013 May). Personal Interview. Anderson, Indiana.

Kobrowski, N.R. (1972-2013). Personal Experience. Lake home in Anderson, Indiana.

Kobrowski, N.R. (1981). Investigation. Anderson, Indiana: Dickey Road.

Kobrowski, N.R. (1988). Investigation. Pendleton, Indiana: Falls Park.

Kobrowski, N.R. (2008). Haunted Backroads: Central Indiana (and other stories). (Westfield, IN: Unseenpres.com, Inc.).

Kobrowski, N.R. (2013). Investigation. Anderson, Indiana: Killbuck Park.

Kobrowski, N.R. (2013). Investigation. Anderson, Indiana: Moss Island.

Kobrowski, N.R. (1988). Personal Experience. Anderson, Indiana: East Lynn House.

Kobrowski, N.R. (2013). Investigation. Anderson, Indiana: N CR5050 W

Kobrowski, N.R. (2013). Investigation. Anderson, Indiana: Old Walmart

Kobrowski, N.R. (2013). Personal Experience. Anderson, Indiana: Priest House.

Kobrowski, N.R. (2013). Personal Experience. Anderson, Indiana: St. Mary's School and Church.

Kobrowski, N.R. (2013). If You Grew Up in Anderson, IN. Retrieved September 2, 2013 from https://www.facebook.com/groups/249146618437655/per-malink/646145122071134/

Kobrowski, N.R. (2008). The Encyclopedia of Haunted Indiana (Westfield, IN: Unseenpres.com, Inc.).

Kobrowski, N.R. & Kobrowski, M.K. (2006). Investigation. Anderson, Indiana: Anderson High School (aka Madison Heights High School).

Kobrowski, N.R. & Kobrowski, M.K. (2006). Investigation. Wilkerson, Indiana: Hays Cemetery.

Kobrowski, N.R. & Kobrowski, M.K. (2013). Investigation. Anderson, Indiana: Camp Chesterfield.

Kobrowski, N.R. & Kobrowski, M.K. (2013). Investigation. Pendleton, Indiana: Falls Park.

Kobrowski, N.R. & Kobrowski, M.K. (2013). Investigation. Anderson, Indiana: Fraternal Order of Eagles.

Kobrowski, N.R. & Kobrowski, M.K. (2013). Investigation. Frankton, Indiana: French Cemetery

Kobrowski, N.R. (2013). Investigation. Pendleton, Indiana: Grovelawn Cemetery

Kobrowski, N.R. & Kobrowski, M.K. (2011). Investigation. Anderson, Indiana: Dickey Road.

Kobrowski, N.R. & Kobrowski, M.K. (2013). Investigation. Anderson, Indiana: Gruenewald Home.

Kobrowski, N.R. & Kobrowski, M.K. (2013). Investigation. Anderson, Indiana: Grand Avenue.

Kobrowski, N.R. & Kobrowski, M.K. (2013). Investigation. Anderson, Indiana: Maplewood Cemeteries.

Kobrowski, N.R. & Kobrowski, M.K. (2013). Investigation. Anderson, Indiana: Marshall House.

Kobrowski, N.R. & Kobrowski, M.K. (2013). Investigation. Anderson, Indiana: Shadyside Park.

Kobrowski, N.R. & Kobrowski, M.K. (2013). Investigation. Frankton, Indiana: Sigler Cemetery

Kobrowski, N.R. & Kobrowski, M.K. (2006). Investigation. Anderson, Indiana: Vineyard House.

Kobrowski, N.R. & Kobrowski, M.K. (1972-2013). Personal Experience. Anderson, Indiana.

Kokomo Tribune. (1993). Obituaries: Roy Fennessy. Retrieved May 2, 2013 from http://kokomo.newspaperarchive.com/kokomo-tribune/1993-05-10/page-8

Kreegar, R.E (2011) Sansberry instrumental in creation of Mounds State Park. Retrieved May 2, 2013 from http://heraldbulletin.com/peopleand-places/x1075334087/Sansberry-instrumental-in-creation-of-Mounds-State-Park

Lila*, (2002, December). Personal Interviews. Anderson, Indiana.

Long, S & Long, S. (2013 May). Personal Interview. Anderson, Indiana.

Lozen (2005). Personal Interview. Indianapolis, Indiana

Madison County Historical Society. (2009, August 10) Records: Records Available for Orphans. Retrieved May 2, 2013 from http://mchs09.wordpress.com/records/

Main Street Graveyard. (2005). Original Tales. Retrieved February 20, 2005, from http://originaltales.com/urban/Listings.php?City=P&State=IN&-Type=3

Maplewood Cemetery (n.d.) History. Retrieved May 2, 2013 from http://www.maplewoodcemetery.com/history.asp

Marshall, K. (2013 June). Personal Interview. Alexandria, Indiana.

Mary. (2013 May). Personal Interview. Indianapolis, Indiana.

Mays, M. (2006). Personal Email Interview. Indiana.

Miller, B. & Miller, B. (2012). Personal Interview. Anderson, Indiana.

Moffitt (Schrader), E. (2013). If You Grew Up in Anderson, IN Retrieved July 3, 2013 from https://www.facebook.com/groups/249146618437655/perma-link/620681554617491/

Morbidrequiem. (2006, August 1). 01 August 2006 [August 1, 2006 message]. Message posted to http://morbidrequiem.livejournal.com/

Mt. Gilliad. (2005). Original Tales. Retrieved February 20, 2005 from http://originaltales.com/urban/Listings.php?City=P&State=IN-Type=3

Nancy. (2013 May). Personal Interview. Anderson, Indiana.

Native American Forest Mythology. (n.d.). Retrieved May 2, 2013 from http://www.native-languages.org/legends-forest.htm

Nivens, M.A. (2013 May). Personal Interview. Anderson, Indiana.

Pendleton Business Association (n.d.). History of Pendleton, Indiana. Retrieved June 2, 2013 from http://www.pendletonin.org/index.php/about-pend-leton-indiana.html

Pioneer Cemeteries and Their Stories, Madison County, Indiana (n.d.). Abbott Cemetery. Retrieved May 2, 2013 from http://www.cemeteries-madison-co-in.com/abbott_cemetery.htm

Pioneer Cemeteries and Their Stories, Madison County, Indiana (n.d.). Bronnenberg Cemetery. Retrieved May 2, 2013 from http://www.cemeteries-madison-co-in.com/bron-nenberg.htm

Pioneer Cemeteries and Their Stories, Madison County, Indiana (n.d.). West

Maplewood Cemetery. Retrieved May 2, 2013 from http://www.cemeter-ies-madison-co-in.com/west_maplewood_cemetery.htm
Renee* (2005). Personal Interview. Indianapolis, Indiana.
Richard. (2012, March). Personal Interview. Anderson, Indiana.
Richey, L. (2006, January). Personal Interview. Telephone Interview, Indiana.
Richey, L. (2013, June). Personal Interview. Telephone Interview, Indiana.
Richey, M. (2013, June). Personal Interview. Telephone Interview, Indiana.
Richey, M. (2006, January). Personal Interview. Telephone Interview, Indiana.
Sam. (2013 May). Personal Interview. Anderson, Indiana.
Sherrie. (2013, May). Personal Interview. Anderson, Indiana.
Smith, B. (2012 December) Personal Interview. Anderson, Indiana.
The Elwood Call Leader. "Haunted House" The Elwood Call Leader.53 Aug 1910: 1. Print.
The Elwood Call Leader. "Haunted House on North West Side" The Elwood Call Leader. (n.d.): 5. Print.
The Elwood Call Leader. "Noisy Spooks Invisible" The Elwood Call Leader. 23 May 1914: 11. Print.
The Elwood Daily Record. "A Ghost Story From West Side Is A Thriller" The Elwood Daily Record. 5 Aug 1910: 1. Print.
The Elwood Daily Record. "Ghost Story Denied" The Elwood Daily Record 8 Aug 1910: 5. Print.
The Elwood Daily Record. "Haunted Cottage" The Elwood Daily Record 11 Sep 1903. Print.
The Lake* Family, (2002, December). Personal Interviews. Lake home in Anderson, Indiana.
The Skeptic's Dictionary. (2010). Camp Chesterfield. Retrieved May 2, 2013 from http://www.skepdic.com/chesterfield.htm
The Technical Association of the Pulp and Paper Industry. (1918). Death of Samuel A. Cook.
Thompson, C. (2013). If You Grew Up in Anderson, IN Retrieved July 3, 2013 from https://www.facebook.com/groups/249146618437655/perma-link/620681554617491/
Timmons, Matthew (2013 May). Personal Interview. Telephone Interview. Indianapolis, Indiana.
Town of Pendleton Indiana (2013). History of Pendleton. Retrieved June 2, 2013 from http://www.town.pendleton.in.us/history-of-pendleton.cfm

Unknown. (n.d.). Sylvester Family Genealogy. Madison County Historical Society.

Unknown. (n.d.) One-Mile House. Undated print.

Ward, Y.W.W (2003). A Brief History of Camp chesterfield. Retrieved May 2, 2013 from http://www.campchesterfield.net/Camp_Chesterfield_A_Spiritual_Center_of_Light/A_Brief_History_of_Camp_Chesterfield.htm

Wesco, Z. (2013 June). Personal Interview. Alexandria, Indiana.

Whitsell-Sherman, J. (2013, May) Personal Interview. Telephone Interview. Anderson, Indiana.

Whitsell-Sherman, J. (2013, June) Personal Interview. Telephone Interview. Anderson, Indiana.

Index

Final Word

The author loves hearing from her readers. If you wish to contact Nicole Kobrowski, she can be reached via email at customerservice@ unseenpress.com.

She invites you to join the Unseenpress.com, Inc. Facebook page: **http://www.facebook.com/ghosttoursIN**

You can also join her author page at: **https://www.facebook.com/ pages/Nicole-Kobrowski/234356579933272**

Nicole is always up for a good ghost story!

CPSIA information can be obtained
at www.ICGtesting.com
Printed in the USA
LVHW082259290719
625809LV00015B/1038/P